Hallowed FIRE

FAITH MOTIVATION OF EARLY WOMEN ACTIVISTS

CARMA VAN LIERE

Judson Press ® Valley Forge

agd 2198

Library of Congress Cataloging-in-Publication Data

Van Liere, Carma, 1918–
    Hallowed fire : faith motivation of early women activists / by
Carma Van Liere.
        p.   cm.
    Includes bibliographical references.
    ISBN 0-8170-1160-9
    1. Feminism—United States—History.   2. Women social reformers—
United States—History.   3. Feminism—Religious aspects—
Christianity.   4. Women—United States—Religious life.   I. Title.
HQ1426.V36   1991
305.42′0973—dc20   91-13363
                                                                          CIP

Foreword

Several years ago I wrote a little book about biblical equality for women in the church. I set out to find answers to questions that had nagged at me for years. Even before *Woman Be Free* was finished, women began seeking me out to ask, Could it be true? Could it be possible, that in God's eyes, women really are equal with men?

Over and over, the same thing happened. My questioners were transformed before my eyes as they listened to proof after proof. It was as if they had been freed and were suddenly more vitally alive. Now they *knew* they were wholly human, wholly desired by God, wholly freed, and fully utilizable for sevice. I can never forget those joyful awakenings.

But the reason my questioners could respond that way was because of where they came from. They came from the same place most Christian women find themselves. They believed, because they had been taught to by people they trusted, that they were second-class persons in the church and in society. Efforts to ask the kinds of questions that sent me searching had been effectively squelched, and their concerns for equality dismissed as merely the selfish echo of a secular movement.

Those women, like all of us, need two things in order to stand tall and walk free. They, and we, need to know the Bible itself—what it says about us and what it means for us. Then we need to know our history, and experience its empowering effects. Both will astonish us, for not only are we fully free in God's sight, but we have a fine and honorable past that is now coming to light.

In the pages of this book that good light shines. It is time we warmed ourselves in it and then spread it about. Not all of the people who have tried to restrict and inhibit the equal participation of women have done so out of malice. Not all of those who have dismissed our efforts toward equal opportunity as an accomodation to a secular feminist movement have been uncaring. Many are simply ignorant. Now you will have the facts to enlighten them.

I am particularly pleased to introduce such a readable and accessible book. It will go a long way toward providing Christian women the sense of self-respect and possibility awareness they need. We have a glowing past and a bright future.

Patricia Gundry

Contents

CHAPTER ONE

Of Brooms and Firebrands

Today's women often have the idea that the "women's movement" began just a few years ago, in the 1960s, and that it is godless, destructive of the family, and dangerous even to think about, let alone to put into practice. Let us take a look at the last one hundred and fifty years or so and see how in truth it all began.

An early women's rights activist, author, and abolitionist, Lydia Maria Child, writing in 1837, vividly described what was then happening to many Christian women in America. She made use of a well-known fable, the story of the sorcerer's apprentice. The sorcerer had cast a spell on a broom so as to render it able to carry water from a nearby river. In this way, the sorcerer's apprentice would not have to do the heavy work. When his employer was not around, the apprentice decided to try the spell himself. At first he was overjoyed to find that he could, indeed, command the broom to do his bidding—but then he realized that he did not know how to turn it back into a broom. All the tubs were full of water and the creature continued to carry more, while the frightened apprentice cried out, "Stop! Stop! We shall all be drowned, if you don't stop!"

Child compared the situation in the fable to "those who urged women to become missionaries, and to form tract societies." Women who saw themselves as having a call to spread the gospel had what Child called "prodigious influence, and consequent responsibility" and their "sympathies and thoughts" became "active and enlarged far beyond the bounds of the hearth and the nursery." Thus, "the sects called evangelical were the first agitators of the woman question."[1]

What happened then, as we shall see from many examples, was that many Christian women realized that they could, like men, study and learn, speak in public in defense of their faith, raise money for worthy causes, and work to change laws and social conditions that were exploiting others. But many of the men of the church were beginning to think that it was time to turn the apprentice's apprentice back into a broom. This feeling that "the woman question" has gotten out of hand continues to the present day. How did it all start? And does the Christian woman have to be turned back into a broom, or can we and must we use all this energy and talent in constructive ways? Let us look at one example of how the "broom" got into the act and how some of the men viewed the situation as having become completely out of control.

The title *Hallowed Fire* is adapted from a speech made in the New York legislature in 1854 in opposition to petitions presented by Susan B. Anthony. The legislator, identified only as "Mr. Burnett, of Essex,"[2] urged the House to consider that "the object of these unsexed females is to overthrow the most sacred of our institutions" and "to set the whole community ablaze with unhallowed fire." Let us see what these terrible steps were that Miss Anthony wanted the legislature to take and whether the storm that arose reminds us of anything in our own day, over one hundred and thirty-five years later.

Susan B. Anthony was thirty-four years old at the time of this frightening attack on all that Mr. Burnett held dear. A single woman all her life, Anthony was a Quaker, quiet and dignified—patently the opposite of the "unsexed female" (one assumes that Mr. Burnett had in mind a woman who wanted so much to be a man that there was nothing feminine about her) who was going to set the whole community ablaze in such a terrifying way.

Starting out as a school teacher, Anthony early became aware of the inequities in conditions of employment for women. Several times she was assigned to rural schools in which male teachers had been dismissed because of their incompetence. She succeeded where they had failed, but was paid, as was customary, only one-fourth the salary the man had been receiving.

After leaving the schoolroom, she became actively interested in the temperance movement and began to see that little could be done about the evils of strong drink so long as women, the main champions of the cause, had little power and no money of their own. Thus, votes for women and some control over their own resources became her main goals.

In 1854, Susan B. Anthony went to the New York State legislature to present two petitions signed by thousands of women. The first asked that a married woman gain (a) control over whatever wages she earned, and (b) equal rights over the guardianship of her children. The second petition asked for voting rights for women.

After lengthy debate, the legislative committee returned a recommendation that (a) the wife be allowed to collect and control her own earnings if the family were neglected by the husband, and (b) her written consent be required for the apprenticeship of her children. But it rejected the petition for voting rights.

The already mentioned speech in opposition to these recommendations deserves to be quoted at length as representing some of the misguided thinking of the age, and will bear thinking about in connection with some of the rhetoric concerning the women's movement today:

> I hope before even this motion is put the gentlemen will be allowed to reflect upon the important question whether these individuals deserve any consideration at the hands of the Legislature. Whatever may be their pretensions or their sincerity, they do not appear satisfied with having unsexed themselves, but they want to unsex every female in the land, and to set the whole community ablaze with unhallowed fire. I trust, sir, the House may deliberate before we suffer them to cast their firebrand into

our midst. True, as yet, there is nothing officially before us; but it is well to know that the object of these unsexed females is to overthrow the most sacred of our institutions, to set at defiance the divine law which declares man and wife to be one; and establish on its ruins what will be in fact and in principle but a species of legalized adultery.

Are we to put the stamp of truth upon the libel here set forth, that men and women in the matrimonial relation are to be equal? We know that God created man to be the representative of the race; that after his creation his Creator took from his side the material for woman's creation; and that, by the institution of matrimony, woman was restored to the side of man, and they became one flesh and one being, he the Head. But should this mischievous scheme be carried to its legitimate results, we instead of reposing safe confidence against assaults upon our honor in the love and affection of our wives, shall find ourselves obliged to close the approaches to those assaults by the padlock.[3]

He was trying to put the broom back into the closet. All this rhetoric, let us remember, was in response, not to a demand for free love, but to the request that married women who worked in mills, gave music lessons, sewed dresses for other women, and the like, be entitled to their own earnings. As it was, the law gave their husbands the money, with the privilege of spending or saving it as they wished. And, as if the control of their own money were not shocking enough, these crazy women wanted to be consulted on decisions about the future of their children. Apprenticeship might be a very good training, or it might amount almost to slavery, a term of service in which the young person was worked very hard and treated very badly. Was the flame with which the wives and mothers were ablaze holy or unholy?

It has been over one hundred and thirty-five years since that speech was made, but almost every proposal since then for giving women rights and responsibilities that are equal to those of men has been suggested by those who want women to be free to do God's will. Ironically, many of those who have opposed women's rights—people who are trying to put the broom back into the closet—also claim to be doing the will of God.

Notes

1. Reuther, Rosemary and Eleanor McLaughlin, *Women of Spirit: Female Leadership in the Jewish and Christian Traditions* (New York: Simon and Schuster, 1979), p. 280.
2. Ida Husted Harper, *The Life and Work of Susan B. Anthony,* vol. 1 (Indianapolis: Bowen-Merrill Co., 1899), p. 109.
3. Ibid.

CHAPTER TWO

The Road to Seneca Falls

What was going on about one hundred and fifty years ago that prompted Lydia Child to think of herself and her Christian women friends as having escaped from the closet in a burst of vitality like that of the newly energized broom?

In the 1820s and 1830s, especially in the northern part of the young United States, an exciting and contagious spirit of reform was in the air for both men and women. It started in the churches and was involved at first with such Christian and humanitarian issues as temperance, missions, and public education. Even though women were not supposed to have any ideas other than those of their fathers or husbands, and even on these ideas were not to speak out in public, Christian women were beginning to play an important part in these reform movements.

The cause that especially appealed to many Christian women in the early 1800s was the abolition of slavery. At the 1838 meeting of the American Anti-Slavery Society, a group formed in Philadelphia in 1833, four women were scheduled to speak—a highly unusual agenda in that day. They were Angelina Grimké, Abby Kelley, Lucretia Mott (whom we shall see again in 1848), and Maria Chapman. Before an audience of three thousand, the famous William Lloyd Garrison was addressing the crowd when a mob gathered outside Pennsylvania Hall, broke windows, and drowned out the speaker with "howls and shouts of derision."[1] The mob was dispersed, and the next day the women were willing to try it again, but the mayor, concerned for their safety, forbade the meeting to be held. The whole fuss was partly because of objections to the antislavery movement and partly because of the presence of women.

The four women then proceeded to organize a Philadelphia Female Anti-Slavery Society, including in its constitution the statement that "slavery and prejudice against color are contrary to the laws of God."²

In Article XII of the Constitution of the Society, we read, "It is especially recommended that the members of this Society should entirely abstain from purchasing the products of slave labor, that we may be able consistently to plead the cause of our brethren in bonds."³ The products involved were such things as sugar and cotton, not easy items to avoid. This is a very early example of economic boycott as a weapon of peaceful dissent, carried out by women who, then as now, largely decided what would be purchased for family consumption.

By the end of the thirties, female antislavery societies existed in New York, Ohio, Indiana, and Illinois, as well as in the Michigan Territory. In 1837 the first Anti-Slavery Convention of American Women was held in New York City, attended by more than two hundred women. In their resolution was this statement:

> Resolved that as certain rights and duties are common to all moral beings, the time has come for woman to move into that sphere which Providence has assigned her, and no longer remain satisfied in the circumscribed limits with which corrupt custom and *a perverted application of Scripture* have encircled her; therefore it is the duty of woman, and the province of woman, to plead the cause of the oppressed in our land, and to do all that she can by her voice, and her pen, and her purse, and the influence of her example, to overthrow the horrible system of American slavery.⁴

Anyone who feels that the concept of "female" societies of any kind is degrading must be reminded that women did not, up to this time, have any voice or any vote in the societies already in existence, which were governed 100 percent by men.

Lydia Child wrote a precedent-setting book entitled *An Appeal in Favor of the Class of Americans Called Africans.* Published in 1833, it was the first antislavery book published in the United States. Child had done a great deal of research in the Atheneum Library in Boston, where she was one of very few women to have a coveted user's card. The book told of mass kidnappings and forced marches in Africa and journeys to the United States in nightmare slave galleys. It then surveyed state laws on slavery and described the brutalized lives of the slaves. "We say," she noted, "Negroes are so ignorant that they must be kept slaves and we insist on keeping them ignorant, lest we spoil them as slaves." Any sign of independent action by a slave was punished by whippings, sometimes by death.

The book, understandably, aroused a storm of protest. Her prized library card was withdrawn, and subscriptions to her thriving magazine, *The Juvenile Miscellany,* the first magazine in the United States for children, declined so much that it ceased publication. Mrs. M. J. C. Mason, wife of the Virginia senator who drew up the Fugitive Slave Law, wrote to Child to explain how kind the slave owners were to the slaves, alleviating the suffering of the dying, and "softening the pangs of maternity." Child wrote back that the Northern women she knew also sewed for the poor and watched over the sick, and "I have never known an instance where the 'pangs of maternity' did not meet with requisite assistance; and here at the North, after we have helped the mothers, *we do not sell the babies.* "[5]

Angelina Grimké and her sister Sarah were women brought up in the South who came to see the evils of slavery very clearly. Angelina's "Appeal to the Christian Women of the South," written in 1836, was widely distributed. She urged the women to read the Bible and judge for themselves whether Jesus would have sanctioned "oppression and crime." After prayerful consideration, they were to act in civil disobedience, such as teaching the slaves to read. Then she went on to state eloquently that women have always acted as leaders when God called on them to do so:

> Are there no women in that noble array of martyrs who are now singing the song of Moses and the Lamb? Who led the women of Israel from the house of bondage, striking the timbrel and singing the song of deliverance on the banks of that sea whose waters stood up like walls of crystal to open a passage for their escape? It was a woman, Miriam, the prophetess. . . . Who first proclaimed Christ as the true Messiah in the streets of Samaria? . . . It was a *woman!*[6]

Angelina Grimké's "Appeal" is included in the Appendix. The aspect of it that we need to consider here is that the biblical bases for Christian feminism that today seem so innovative were known and quoted almost one hundred fifty years ago!

On the other hand there were then, as now, blasts from the pulpits condemning these women. Many clergymen saw any kind of female leadership role as very threatening—as the broom beginning indeed to bring enough water to drown them all. In 1837 a pastoral letter was read from all the Congregational pulpits in New England that said, among other things, "The appropriate duties and influence of women are clearly stated in the New Testament. . . . The power of woman is in her dependence, flowing from the consciousness of that weakness which God has given her for her protection."[7] A woman praying at prayer meetings and teaching in "Sabbath-schools" was all right, but "when woman assumes the place and tone of man as a public reformer" the church "cannot but regret" her mistaken conduct.

Sarah Grimké, Angelina's sister, in response to the pastoral letter, wrote "On the Woman Question," one of the earliest and most influential statements on women's rights. In Letter I we read, "Here I plant myself; God created us equal— he created us free agents;—he is our Lawgiver, our King and our Judge, and to him and to him alone is woman bound to be in subjection, and to him alone is she accountable for the use of those talents with which her Heavenly Father has entrusted her."[8] Grimké compared the pastoral letter to the witch trials of the seventeenth century, which "solemnly condemned nineteen persons and one dog to death for witchcraft!" She then went on to say, "I am inclined to think, when we [women] are admitted to the honor of studying Greek and Hebrew, we shall produce some various readings of the Bible a little different from those we now have."[9] This did indeed turn out to be true.

White women opposed slavery out of altruism, but there were other movements, such as education for women and the right to vote, which involved women's concern for their self-interests. One of these, which we shall consider in detail later, was the temperance movement—an effort to outlaw all alcoholic beverages. Because of the social and economic impact of alcoholism on the family, this was a cause to which thousands of Christian women devoted their time, their money (if any), and their new-found talents for organizing and speaking.

So we see that the first third of the nineteenth century found women becoming increasingly conscious of and vocal about causes opposing exploitation of other human beings. As they learned to organize and work together, they were occasionally successful in getting a law passed, which of course involved getting the cooperation of men, since only men could vote.

Every century has its list of women who were either canonized or martyred—or both. But suddenly it seemed there were thousands of American women from all walks of life beginning to burn with the hallowed fire of the realization that God had work for them to do beyond the bounds of the hearth and the nursery.

Notes

1. Alice Felt Tyler, *Freedom's Ferment: Phases of American Social History from the Revolution to the Outbreak of the Civil War* (New York: Torchbooks-Harper & Row, Publishers Inc., 1962), p. 504.
2. Judith Papachristou, *Women Together: A History in Documents of the Women's Movement in the United States* (New York: Alfred Knopf, 1976), p. 4.
3. Ibid., p 5.
4. Ibid., p. 7. Author's emphasis.
5. Margaret Farrant Thorp, *Female Persuasion: Six Strong-Minded Women* (New Haven, Conn.: Yale University Press, 1949), p. 229.
6. Papachristou, *Women Together,* p. 10.
7. Ibid., p. 12.
8. Ibid., p. 13.
9. Ibid.

CHAPTER THREE

Seneca Falls

In the summer of 1848, several hundred men and women traveled to the small town of Seneca Falls, New York, for what we now know to be a precedent-setting convention.

It is convenient to begin the discussion of any great movement in history by assigning a single event or date as the starting point. If we state flatly that the women's movement in the United States began with the first Women's Rights Convention in Seneca Falls, we immediately meet a great many comments such as, "Well, yes . . . but! But how about the women who were speaking up for the religious, political, and civil rights of American women before 1848?"

In very much the same way, the religious historian who dates the beginning of the Protestant Reformation from Luther's nailing of the Ninety-five Theses to the church door at Wittenberg in 1517 has to answer those who say, "Yes, but . . . how about those who came before Luther, such as Wycliffe and Huss?" And the literary historian who dates the beginning of the Romantic Movement in English poetry from the publication of Wordsworth and Coleridge's *Lyrical Ballads* in 1798 has to deal somehow with poets such as Burns and Blake, who flourished as romantic writers somewhat earlier.

The fact is that nothing springs into being full grown, but there is often a significant statement, such as the Ninety-five Theses or the Preface to the *Lyrical Ballads,* that serves as a catalyst. Those who have been expressing some kind of dissatisfaction or rebellion, singly or in small groups, over a period of time or a portion of the world find in such a statement a rallying cry around which to unite and around which a movement can be formed.

It was just such a catalyst that was formed when five women sat down at a mahogany table (which is now in the Smithsonian Institution) to draw up an agenda for the world's first Women's Rights Convention. It was to be held July 19 and 20, 1848, in the Wesleyan Chapel in Seneca Falls. The five women were Elizabeth Cady Stanton, Lucretia Mott, Martha C. Wright (Lucretia's younger sister), Jane Hunt, and Mary Elizabeth McClintock.[1] All except Stanton were Quakers. Like the soldiers at the bridge in Emerson's poem, they were about to fire shots that would be heard round the world—or at least across the nation—and that would continue to echo through time down to the present day.

They were not, of course, the first women in history to consider the issues that they were about to tackle. The cause that had first brought some of them together was the abolition of slavery, a cause to which, as we have seen, many Christians rallied, including many women. Lucretia Mott and Elizabeth Stanton met for the first time in 1840 in London at a World Anti-Slavery Convention, to which Lucretia Mott and Henry Stanton, Elizabeth's new husband, were sent as United States delegates.

The British had issued a call for the Convention without specifying that the delegates be male. The Pennsylvania and Massachusetts antislavery societies sent large delegations, including women. When the convention in London opened, the women delegates were not allowed to sit in the voting section at the business meetings. Understandably, this created a floor fight, and as always, biblical backing was offered by both sides. The women were urged to withdraw voluntarily, thus avoiding the issue of disqualification. They did not, but when the vote was taken, women were excluded by an overwhelming majority. William Lloyd Garrison expressed his disapproval by sitting with the rejected women in the gallery.[2]

Then and there, Stanton and Mott began a lifelong friendship and began to think about a convention of their own at which the "social, civil, and religious conditions and rights of women" (to quote from the newspaper notice that was to appear later) would be discussed. Probably because of their family commitments—Lucretia was already, in 1840, the mother of five, and Elizabeth gave birth to three sons between 1841 and 1845—their plans did not materialize for eight years after their memorable meeting in London.

The year 1848, as Miriam Gurko points out, "was marked by revolutions and reform, by popular stirrings and new beginnings."[3] The discovery of gold in California sparked westward migration, and the people of the frontier believed in a social equality that influenced all of American life. The same year, Dorothea Dix, after ten years of tirelessly investigating and publicizing the terrible conditions in mental hospitals, finally persuaded Congress to pass the first bill providing federal support for these institutions. Although vetoed by President Pierce, the bill was the forerunner of much reform legislation to follow. In New York State, the Married Woman's Property Act was passed, giving married women some degree of control over their property. Before this law, a husband automatically took possession of any property which his wife brought into the marriage. The passage of this law no doubt was encouraged by fathers who wished to pass on property to their married daughters and grandchildren without the intervention of sons-in-law who might prove to be irresponsible or dishonest.

In 1848 anesthesia was first used in childbirth, despite opposition from clergymen who said that it was flying in the face of God's will, which was for women to bring forth children in sorrow. (One wonders if any sermons were preached on the sinfulness of using farm animals and equipment to make easier the task of the man—after all, he had been told that he would have to till the earth by the sweat of his brow!)

One of the almost incredible aspects of the first Women's Rights Convention was that the only publicity it received was a notice of less than a hundred words in the Seneca County *Courier,* a newspaper with a very limited circulation. Yet three hundred people, mostly women, attended—this at a time when women usually did not travel (or do anything else) without the men in their lives, and when travel of any kind was difficult and time-consuming. The announcement read:

> WOMEN'S RIGHTS CONVENTION—a convention to discuss the social, civil, and religious rights of woman will be held in the Wesleyan Chapel, at Seneca Falls, N.Y., on Wednesday and Thursday the 19th and 20th of July, current, commencing at 10 o'clock A.M. During the first day, the meeting will be exclusively for women, who are earnestly invited to attend. The public, generally, are invited to be present on the second day, when Lucretia Mott, of Philadelphia, and other ladies and gentlemen, will address the convention.[4]

A young woman, Charlotte Woodward, who, incidentally, was the only woman present at the convention who survived to cast her vote in 1920 in the first presidential election open to women voters, told many years later of her impressions of the convention. She herself wanted to be a typesetter and work in a print shop, a career not then considered suitable for a woman. She read the *Courier* notice and ran to her neighbors, to find that others were as excited about the convention as she. With half a dozen of her friends, she set forth early in the morning in a wagon drawn by farm horses, wondering if any other women would be there. As they came closer to Seneca Falls, they met many vehicles going to the same destination. The audience of some three hundred included about forty men, in spite of the original restriction that the first day was to be for women only.

Charlotte was among the sixty-eight women and thirty-two men who signed their names at the end of the convention to the Declaration of Sentiments.

The agenda for the convention consisted of a Declaration of Sentiments and a list of twelve resolutions. The complete text, consisting of about fifteen hundred words, has been reproduced in the Appendix and is well worth reading in its entirety. What I wish to do is to emphasize the way in which the whole Declaration reflects the women's faith in God and their clear perception (not by any means universally realized in the 1980s!) that their religious condition and rights went along, and were not at all incompatible, with their social and civil rights. The Declaration was based on the Declaration of Independence and began in almost the same words:

> When in the course of human events, it becomes necessary for one portion of the family of man to assume among the people of the earth a position different from that which they have hitherto occupied, but one to which the laws of nature and of nature's God entitle them, a decent respect for the opinions of mankind requires that they should declare the causes that impel them to such a course.

Then it goes on, again in imitation of the Declaration of Independence: "We hold these truths to be self-evident; that all men and women are created equal; that they are endowed by their Creator with certain inalienable rights. . . ."

Among these inalienable rights are the vote—remember, this did not come to pass on the national level until the Nineteenth Amendment became law in 1920—and, especially for married women, rights to property and wages, right to the guardianship of a woman's own children in case of divorce or separation, and the right to an education. The sections applying mainly to religious life are:

> He [man] allows her in Church, as well as in State, but a subordinate position, claiming Apostolic authority for her exclusion from the ministry, and, with some exceptions, from any public participation in the affairs of the Church. [Again], he has usurped the prerogative of Jehovah himself, claiming it as his right to assign for her a sphere of action, when that belongs to her conscience and to her God.

These were, indeed, not women who did not know the Bible; these were women who had read it for themselves and come up with different concepts from the men who purported to speak for them. It was, in fact, a reformation, just as the re-examination of the teachings of the Catholic church in light

of the open Bible and the priesthood of believers had led to
the Protestant Reformation some three hundred years earlier.

In the Resolutions, the "Whereas" speaks of the law of
nature "dictated by God himself" and superior to any other
law on earth. The third resolution states the "woman is man's
equal—was intended to be so by the Creator." The eighth
resolution states that "woman has too long rested satisfied in
the circumscribed limits which corrupt customs and a *perverted
application of the Scriptures* have marked out for her, and that it
is time she should move in the enlarged sphere which her
great Creator has assigned her" (author's emphasis).

The summing up begins:

> Resolved, therefore, That being invested by the Creator with the
> same capabilities, and the same consciousness of responsibility
> for their exercise, it is demonstrably the right and duty of woman,
> equally with man, to promote every righteous cause by every
> righteous means, and especially in regard to the great subjects of
> morals and religion, it is self-evidently her right to participate
> with her brother in teaching them both in private and in public,
> by writing and by speaking, by any instrumentalities proper to be
> used, and in any assemblies proper to be held.[5]

Astonishingly, the principles and resolutions were all accepted unanimously, except the ninth resolution, dealing with
the elective franchise, which was hotly debated, and barely
squeaked by. It was defended by Elizabeth Stanton, warmly
supported by Frederick Douglass. This is interesting because,
after the Civil War, one of the most hotly debated issues was
whether women should work for their own vote or step aside
to work first for the franchise of African American men.

As we shall see, the women of Seneca Falls were so far
ahead of their time that not all of their self-evident truths and
inalienable rights are universally accepted by Christians even
today.

Notes

1. Miriam Gurko, *The Ladies of Seneca Falls: The Birth of the Women's Rights Movement* (New York: Macmillan Publishing Co., 1974), p. 2.
2. Alice Felt Tyler, *Freedom's Ferment: Phases of American Social History from the Revolution to the Outbreak of the Civil War* (New York: Torchbooks-Harper & Row, Publishers, Inc., 1962), p. 447.
3. Gurko, *Ladies of Seneca Falls*, pp. 45–51.
4. Ibid., pp. 94–95.
5. Judith Papachristou, *Women Together: A History in Documents of the Women's Movement in the United States* (New York: Alfred Knopf, 1976), pp. 24–26.

CHAPTER FOUR

"Jesus Loves Me, This I Know"

"The Benevolent Empire" is a phrase that has been widely used to describe the vast complex of activities in which American Christian women engaged during the early years of the nineteenth century. The expression is not always used in a favorable sense. Some modern writers use it in a kind of sneering tone, implying that an empire is bad no matter how benevolent it is—somewhat like benign dictatorship. These critics believe that a person is better staggering along on his or her own two feet than being held up by someone else, no matter how kindly the intentions of the emperor.

The activities of this vast "empire" were varied indeed; they included support for free and universal education, health care, orphans' homes, care for the aged and infirm, improved conditions in factories and mines, and campaigns against slavery, war, intoxicating beverages, and prostitution—the list is endless. There was always, of course, the underlying notion that the "benevolent ones" knew what was best for everyone, an attitude that was resented by those who had their own ideas about what was good for them. And sometimes, perhaps, the strong-minded women really did err in the direction of forcing people to live lives of moral purity. One must also admit that all the aspirations of the "empire" were not, and cannot, be achieved.

As Christians, however, we know that we are our brothers' and sisters' keepers. Add to that the belief that we are to

spread the gospel, and the result was home and foreign missionary societies and Sunday schools, both of which have
played an important role in even small and struggling
churches.

As women struggled for abolition and temperance, they
learned invaluable lessons about "social, legal, moral, and
political injustice."[1] On that training ground they found out
what it took to change the system and how they could go
about changing it.

Home missions, like foreign missions, was a term that
included religious instruction as one element on a long list of
projects of care and concern for people who were in unfortunate circumstances. Organizations such as "Relief of Poor
Widows with Small Children" and "Association for the Relief
of Respectable, Aged, Indigent Females" illustrate vividly the
kinds of philanthropies in which nineteenth-century Christian
women were engaged. If they show a tendency toward social
control, they also show an awakening of social consciousness.
Prisons, hospitals, almshouses, sweatshops, slums—all these
and more cried out for reform from Christian women and
men. And middle-class women had the time and the energy
to do something about it. Basic social conditions usually did
not change very much, but individual sufferers were undoubt-
edly provided with "relief"—and not just with promises that
things would be better in the next world.

An example of this endeavor was the founding of a
women's hospital in New York City by Sarah Doremus, whom
we will meet again in the chapter on foreign missions. In her
work with many destitute women who suffered from gyneco-
logical diseases, she saw the need for a health center for poor
women. Because modesty opposed any discussion of female
reproductive organs, raising funds proved to be very difficult.
Finally, Doremus and her friends raised money to purchase a
building and found a physician who believed in their cause,
Unable to administer the project, the physician asked Doremus for help. She formed a working board of directors and
went to Albany, where she obtained a state charter and a

ten-thousand-dollar state appropriation! Women's Hospital greatly expanded the medical services available to poor women in New York City.

Now, let us look at the Sunday school as one of the most successful parts of the Benevolent Empire. At the outset the Sunday school movement was designed to help the children of the very poor; only later was it expanded to include other children. As we shall see, the movement was not completely the domain of women, but they certainly did the larger share of the work. The question is, Did Christians have any right to try to change people's lives? Looking at the movement two hundred years later, we need to consider thoughtfully— wasn't there great value in this effort? Besides caring for the spiritual needs of the children, Sunday schools also addressed their social, educational, and economic problems. Wasn't it to the advantage of the child of the working-class family to see himself or herself as potentially cleaner, better educated, better mannered, more ambitious, with more hope for the future—because of the values learned in early childhood on Sunday morning?

At a time when the poor, both at home and on the foreign field, were *supposed* to be dirty, undernourished, uneducated, unwell, and doomed to stay in their "place," missionaries and Sunday school teachers were on the whole a good influence to bring about changes for the better. The child of the poor was not much better off than a slave, working long hours in a cotton mill, for example. A Saturday night bath and an opportunity on Sunday to learn to read and write, an hour spent in a room with other friendly children and (it is to be hoped) a friendly and sympathetic adult who told the child of Jesus' love could open up new vistas of a life in which conditions could be better.

History records scattered earlier instances of Sabbath schools here and there, but the recognized beginning of the Sunday school as we know it took place in Gloucester, England, in the 1780s. Robert Raikes saw the children of the poor working long hours in factories six days of the week and roaming the streets on Sundays, engaging in what today we would call juvenile delinquency. Raikes wanted to help these youngsters, whose future was indeed bleak if they (a) never learned to read and write, and (b) got into trouble with the law before they were fully grown. As a Christian and the publisher of a Gloucester newspaper, he became interested in jail reform, and thus in the causes of criminal behavior. He began to see a cause-and-effect relationship between ignorance and crime and considered, as today's sociologists would agree, that at least the rudiments of education were necessary to help boys and girls develop the self-esteem and the skills needed for them to lead law-abiding and useful lives.

His idea of bringing the children in off the streets on Sundays to teach them to read was greeted in some quarters with derision. Raikes was called Bobby Wildgoose because he was on this ridiculous wild goose chase. His opponents said these children were not capable of learning, and, anyway, God intended some people to be and remain at the bottom of the heap: the rich man at his table, the poor man at the gate—you know who made them high or lowly!

But Bobby Wildgoose went ahead with his plans. The first classes were held in the teachers' homes, and children were enticed into coming by offers of food and even small sums of money. Raikes wrote about the successes in his Gloucester newspaper. The idea spread. In 1785, William Fox, a London draper [dry goods merchant] and a pious Baptist, formed the first organization for promoting Sunday schools. Its purposes were "to prevent vice, to encourage industry and virtue, to dispel the ignorance of darkness, to diffuse the light of knowledge, to bring men cheerfully to submit to their stations."[2] This illuminating statement shows both the bright side and the dark side of the benevolent empire!

Like some of the other social revolutions, Sunday school must have been an idea whose time had come. The growth of the movement was remarkable. In 1787, only seven years after the first Sunday school, enrollment in England was about

250,000 children. By Raikes's death, thirty-one years after the first school opened, about 500,000 children were attending. Two new elements were very quickly added: (a) in addition to getting the children off the streets and teaching them to read, the schools added religious instruction, and (b) the contributions of women became increasingly important. Sarah Trimmer, a contemporary of Raikes, was an early champion of the Sunday school cause and took it up with Queen Charlotte, wife of George III, of American Revolution fame.

Very soon the idea spread to the United States and was taken up with enthusiasm by American women, ripe in the early 1800s for such activities. In spite of the time involved in getting information across the ocean and the discontinuity caused by the American Revolution, the evangelical community in the New World soon took up the Sunday school cause.

The first Sunday school in New York City was founded in 1793 by an African American woman who had been born a slave. As a child, Catherine (Katy) Ferguson had had a kind mistress who permitted her to attend church services. After a sympathetic woman bought Katy's freedom, she made her living by being a professional cake maker. On Sundays she gathered the neglected children of the neighborhood into her modest home and held school for them. Later arrangements were made for her to use the basement of the Murray Street Church. This was the beginning of the Murray Street Sabbath School, which Mrs. Ferguson conducted for more than forty years. She was interested in teaching the children to read as well as teaching them religion, but she did more than that. She collected forty-eight children from the poorhouse or from destitute parents and either raised them herself or placed them in good homes. Her school was interracial, twenty of her original class being white.[3] In 1920, after she had been dead for seventy years, the Katy Ferguson Home for unwed mothers was founded in New York in tribute to her and in recognition of her early contributions.

Another resident of New York City, Isabella Graham, had

friends and family in Scotland who sent her information about many philanthropic activities, including Sunday schools. Graham and her daughter, Joanna Bethune, took the lead in literally dozens of worthy enterprises, such as the "Society for the Relief of Poor Widows with Small Children." In 1816, Bethune established the Female Union for the Promotion of Sabbath Schools in New York City. Bethune put the word "female" in the name deliberately because she found that men were too slow to respond to her appeals for support. Incidentally, Graham knew Katy Ferguson and invited her and her pupils to her home on at least one occasion.

As in England, the Sunday school movement spread by leaps and bounds. Originally the schools were just for children, and were sometimes the only educational opportunity a child had. It was much later that adult classes were held on Sundays. The schools were at first designed for poor children, but soon children from all economic classes were enrolled.

Assuming that, on the whole, the experience was good for the children, how about the women? Looking back from the last years of the twentieth century, when we tend to think of Sunday school teaching as a responsibility foisted on mostly women and certainly not accorded much status, it is difficult for us to understand how positive the image of the Sunday school teacher was. The work, as well as efforts in other benevolent causes, provided needed opportunities for service and for social interaction beyond the family circle. Boylan quotes from the 1837 minutes of the McKendrean Female Sabbath School Society: "Gratitude becomes us for whom as a sex Christianity has done so much. It has . . . secured us affection, respect, and esteem." Many women looked upon Sunday school work as liberating and enobling.

> For a few, it might even be a stepping-stone to full-time work, whether paid or unpaid, as benevolent society volunteers, missionaries, . . . minister's wives or writers. . . . A large number of . . . women teachers shaped writing careers for themselves by feeding the seemingly insatiable appetites of Sunday school publishers for books and magazine articles.[4]

One of these books, a novel entitled *Say and Seal,* written by two sisters, Anna and Susan Warner, was published in 1860. (Susan was also the author of the best-selling *Wide, Wide World,* which we all remember Jo March "reading and weeping over" in *Little Women.*) The plot of *Say and Seal* deals with the lives of several persons involved in a Sunday school. One of them is a small child, Johnny Fax, who is in very poor health. When his devoted Sunday school teacher comes to see Johnny, it is obvious that the child is dying. Holding up his arms to the teacher, he says, "Sing." The man rocks him and sings a song that Johnny has not heard before. It is "Jesus loves me, this I know, /For the Bible tells me so." Comforted by the song and the caresses, Johnny dies. The following year the words were set to music by William Bradbury, who added the chorus, "Yes, Jesus loves me; the Bible tells me so." This song became the theme song of Sunday schools. The words and music were taught to small children all over the world and translated into countless languages and dialects.[5]

Stories such as *Say and Seal* were typical of the material used by Sunday school teachers in the nineteenth century. Although they seem morbid to us today, they were not so regarded in those days. The child mortality rate at that time was much higher; most families expected to lose several of their children before they reached adulthood. Epidemics of childhood diseases were a fact of life. Just as our materials tend to relate tragedies of broken families or drug and alcohol addiction, their stories were of deaths from consumption or scarlet fever because those were common occurrences.

Sunday school teaching as an activity for women did not usually arouse quite the storm of protest that women in other Christian leadership roles brought forth. However, in Medway, Massachusetts, in 1817, when women suggested the formation of a Sunday school, the deacons rejected the proposal, saying, "These women will be in the pulpit next"![6] They spoke more truly than they knew.

In a typical Sunday school, women's leadership was largely limited to leading others of their sex. For example, a

Sunday school in St. Louis had a staff of fifty-five people in
1868; thirty-eight of them were women. "Although they constituted almost 79 percent of the entire staff and 89 percent
of the teachers, women had no role in running the school or
representing it in public, and eleven of the seventeen men
were officers."[7] The women wiped the runny noses and the
men got their names on the door! The pattern was not
unusual and seemed to be accepted by the evangelical
women.

Organizations of young adults also became increasingly
important in the life of the church: Christian Endeavor, Luther League, Epworth League, Baptist Young People's
Union—the names speak for themselves. Along with the
Young Men's and Young Women's Christian Associations,
they did much to provide religious education and opportunities for companionship and service for youth.

As John Quincy Adams, son of the redoubtable Abigail,
said in the House of Representatives in 1838:

> I say that the correct principle is that women are not only justified
> but exhibit the most exalted virtue, when they . . . depart from
> the domestic circle, and enter upon the concerns of their country,
> of humanity, and of their God.[8]

In entering upon the concerns of their country, of humanity, and of God, Christian women have been instrumental
in an astonishing variety of activities, including not only the
religious education of the young but also the establishment of
hospitals and orphanages, improved conditions in the work
place, humanitarian treatment of the insane, criminals, and
children—the list goes on and on. A Benevolent Empire?
Perhaps, but the empresses were doing what they perceived
as God's will. And God is surely Emperor of the Universe.

Notes

1. Nancy Hardesty, *Women Called to Witness: Evangelical Feminism in the Nineteenth Century* (Nashville: Abingdon Press, 1984), p. 114.
2. Robert W. Lynn and Elliott Wright, *The Big Little School: Two Hundred Years of Sunday School* (Nashville: Abingdon Press, 1980), p. 6.
3. Romeo B. Garrett, *Famous First Facts about Negroes* (Salem, N.H.: Ayer Company Publishers Inc., 1972), p. 189.
4. Anne M. Boylan, *Sunday School: The Formation of an American Institution, 1790–1880* (New Haven, Conn.: Yale University Press, 1988), pp. 121–122.
5. Lynn and Wright, *The Big Little School,* pp. 39–40.
6. Ibid., p. 12.
7. Boylan, *Sunday School,* p. 120.
8. Alice Felt Tyler, *Freedom's Ferment: Phases of American Social History from the Revolution to the Outbreak of the Civil War* (New York: Torchbooks—Harper & Row, Publishers Inc., 1962), p. 429.

CHAPTER FIVE

Louisa and Harriet, for Example

What was life like for women in the first half of the nineteenth century? We can learn something about them from the writings of the women themselves, especially those who were trying to change the status quo, those whose ideas culminated in the statement of principles presented at Seneca Falls.

First of all, there were few opportunities for single women. A woman was not expected to be independent, financially or in any other way; she was expected (and usually she expected) to be regarded all her life as some man's responsibility. If she did not have a husband to continue Papa's care, that job was considered to be her brothers'. Many a young man was prevented for years from marrying because the burden of caring for his unmarried sisters was so great. It was almost, but not quite, unheard of for a father to leave his single daughter money or property in his will, and when he did, it was usually the responsibility of some man in the family to see that she did not use it foolishly. The fact that many young *men* spent their inheritances foolishly was not at all taken into consideration.

One well-known single woman of the nineteenth century was Louisa May Alcott, author of *Little Women* and many other books. The second of four daughters, Louisa could not rely financially on her father, whose career as an educator and author was marked by frequent failed projects. In 1851, when she was nineteen, just three years after Seneca Falls, Louisa

decided to try to support herself and help to contribute to the
support of the family. Her struggle must have been typical of
life for single young women of her time and class.

   She tried teaching, working as a seamstress, and doing a
family's washing for two dollars a week. Then she was asked
by a lawyer to act as a "companion" to his sister. He assured
her that she would be one of the family and do light work
suitable for a gentlewoman. The light work turned out to
include splitting kindling, making fires, taking out the ashes,
and shoveling snow, not even in those days considered work
suitable for a gentlewoman. Finally, when she was asked to
black the master's boots, Louisa quit.[1] A slightly apocryphal
account of Louisa's "going out to service," published in 1880,
says that it was a young theological student who boarded with
the family who asked her to black his boots, to which she
replied that "while studying divinity, he should have learned
humanity." Even if this is not exactly what happened, the
philosophical truth is clear. Christian women, who had been
told all their lives to be meek and humble, suddenly had the
startling idea that Christian men should be considerate of
others and humble themselves.

   For seven weeks of hard work, Louisa received four dollars. Even considering the buying power of a dollar in the
1850s, these were poor wages. As it turned out, she soon
succeeded in making some money with her pen, but of course
this was an option not open to women who did not have
Louisa's gift for writing. Most single women had no choice
but complete dependence on some male relative, or degrading drudgery in someone else's house.

   A married woman's position was regarded as far more
enviable, but the law said that "husband and wife are one and
he is the one." As a rule, wives had no money of their own—a
reason to marvel at what they accomplished in the way of
financial support for causes such as abolition and temperance.
If the husband did not approve of the cause, he would not
give his wife a penny to contribute, and she had scant means
for raising money herself. If she did make any money, for

instance by doing needlework, these funds legally belonged to her husband. Over a long period of time, this law was changed state by state, but only after prolonged, bitter struggles.

As Louisa May Alcott's life illustrated the life of a single woman, the life of Harriet Beecher Stowe will give an idea of life for the married woman in the middle of the century. Because these women were writers, their perceptions of life have been preserved for us. Although their lives were not very much different from those of other women of their day, they do reflect the pattern of what we would call today the "upper middle class"; the lives of women in the mills and factories and in the servant class were a good deal harder (as, of course, were the lives of men who did unskilled labor).

Like most married women in this period, Harriet was the mother of many children, seven in all. In 1838, at the age of twenty-seven, she described her difficulties doing any kind of creative work under these conditions. During her efforts to finish a piece of writing promised to an editor, she first had to do the housecleaning, calm a teething baby, and do a great deal of baking, with only an inexperienced servant girl to help. So she finally sat down at the kitchen table with the baby in her lap and wrote "till it is time to mould up the bread."[2]

A few years later she wrote to her husband, who encouraged her to write but seemed not to do anything to make it easier, that she must have a room of her own to write in. Then he could study in the parlor (he was a professor of theology), and she would not feel that she was interrupting him. She was thirty-nine years old when she wrote *Uncle Tom's Cabin*.

Housework was enormously more difficult than it is today. To do the laundry, for instance, someone had to make the soap, carry and heat the water, soak and scrub the clothes (and bulky clothing it was, too!), hang them out to dry, and iron them with flatirons heated on the kitchen range. Most clothing was made by hand at home, and food was prepared from "scratch." Then remember that all these time-consuming and physically demanding chores were performed by women who spent a good deal of their child-bearing years either pregnant or breast-feeding. Since families were large and life expectancies short, married women did not worry very much about what they were going to do after all their children were grown.

Divorce was rare, but sometimes conditions became so unbearable that a wife would leave an abusive or unfaithful husband, and the law said that the children were his to do with as he pleased. This meant that the wife did not have them to support, as so many single mothers do today, but it also meant that she had no control over what was to become of them. She did not have much control over her children's lives in an ongoing marriage either, as we have seen in the New York State proposal to change the law about apprenticeship; but then, as now, there was some chance to talk over such matters as long as the parents were living together. If they were separated, and the husband so decreed, she might well never see her children again.

Those who are not writers may be saying, "What have Alcott and Stowe to do with me?" We know about writers because they wrote about their own frustrations, but we must also think about the women who would have been inventors, healers, politicians, yes, and preachers, if they had not been told all their lives that those were not roles to which girls could aspire. The loss is not only the loss to the individual woman—what Virginia Woolf calls "some mute and inglorious Jane Austen"—but to the kingdom of God on earth. The need for money of one's own, however small the amount, and a place where one can occasionally be alone—guineas and locks, Woolf calls them—these things have always been, and still are, necessary if a woman is to be creative and thoughtful.

Another source of information about the lives of women in mid-nineteenth-century America is the Declaration of Sentiments presented at Seneca Falls. Just as reading the Declaration of Independence tells us a great deal about the lives of the colonists—as they protested the "quartering large bodies of [British] armed troops among us" and "exciting . . . the

merciless Indian savages against us"—in the Declaration of
Sentiments we read that a woman was "without rights in property, even to the wages she earns." In marriage, the law gave
the husband "power to deprive her of her liberty, and to
administer chastisement."[3] There were battered wives then as
now, the difference being that it was not then against the law!

A woman was prevented, the Declaration went on, from
"nearly all the profitable employments," and all colleges were
closed against her. Even the double standard of morality was
discussed, but not in the worldly sense of "If he can get away
with being sexually promiscuous, why can't I?" Rather, the
sixth "Resolved" says "That the same amount of virtue, delicacy, and refinement of behavior that is required of woman in
the social state, should also be required of man, and the same
transgressions should be visited with equal severity on both
man and woman."[4] The grasp of psychology in the Declaration is remarkable, even in today's terms. "He has endeavored
in every way that he could, to destroy her confidence in her
own powers, to lessen her self-respect, and to make her willing to lead a dependent and abject life."[5]

Notice that none of the resolutions required the newly
liberated woman to reject the Bible. In fact, women were
beginning to see that the Bible had been "perverted" by men,
by inaccurate translations and verses taken out of context.
Properly understood, Scripture, and especially the New Testament, shows women the rights and responsibilities that go
along with being daughters of God. Let us look at the elo-
quent eleventh "Resolved" of the Declaration:

> Resolved, therefore, That, being invested by the Creator with the
> same capabilities, and the same consciousness of responsibility
> for their exercise, it is demonstrably the right and duty of woman,
> equally with man, to promote every righteous cause by every
> righteous means; and especially in regard to the great subjects of
> morals and religion, it is self-evidently her right to participate
> with her brother in teaching them, both in private and in public,
> by writing and by speaking, by any instrumentalities proper to be
> used, and in any assemblies proper to be held; and this being a
> self-evident truth growing out of the divinely implanted princi-

ples of human nature, any custom or authority adverse to it, whether modern or wearing the hoary sanction of antiquity, is to be regarded as a selfevident falsehood, and at war with mankind.[6]

Notes

1. Madeleine Stern, *Behind a Mask: Introduction* (New York: William & Morrow & Co. Inc., 1975), pp. 63–64.
2. Tillie Olsen, *Silences* (New York: Dell Publishing Co., 1989), p. 204.
3. Judith Papachristou, *Women Together: A History in Documents of the Women's Movement in the United States* (New York: Alfred Knopf, 1976), p. 25.
4. Ibid.
5. Ibid.
6. Ibid., p. 26.

CHAPTER SIX

To India's Coral Strand

For her day, and for any time in history, Mary Webb was a remarkable woman. Confined to a wheelchair from the age of five, she got more done than most persons without physical handicaps. In 1800, when she was twenty-one, Webb and twelve other women organized the Boston Female Society for Missionary Purposes. Webb, with sincere "heart, mind, will, prayer, and action,"[1] served as chief organizer. She exerted great influence on the outreach of the Society, but by her own choice never served as its president. For more than forty years, she was its secretary and treasurer.

As Mary Webb was a remarkable woman, the Boston Female Society was a remarkable society. In the first place, it was the first mission support organization in the United States founded and run by women. And it was not strictly denominational. Of the thirteen women at the very first meeting, seven were Baptists and six Congregationalists. In today's world, that does not seem so unusual, but it was highly unusual in 1800, when demoninational lines were very firmly drawn.

Also remarkable was the way in which women were able to raise money for such societies. By law women had no money of their own (if they were married, their resources belonged to their husbands; or if, like Mary Webb, they were single, some male member of the family usually controlled the money), and they could not spend or give away a penny without permission from a male. But somehow they did manage

to produce pennies, and it is astonishing what those pennies
could do. Cent Societies and Mite Societies (referring to the
widow's mite in Luke 21), founded about this time, brought
in enough money to buy incredible quantities of tracts and
Bibles.

It is hard for us to imagine, but in the eyes of many of
Webb's contemporaries, in even so nonthreatening an agency
as a society for the support of foreign missions, leadership
roles were not meant to be held by women. Thus, R. Pierce
Beaver refers to the missionary enterprise as "the first
woman's rights movement in North America." I'm not so sure
about the "firstness," but it was certainly *one* of the first, along
with abolition. And Mary Webb, single, physically handicapped, and active in dozens of other areas including work
with prostitutes, immigrants, and African Americans, "was
able to make inroads where few other women would have
dared venture."[2]

The Boston Female Society for Missionary Purposes was
made up of the women who worked in the United States to
support the missionaries. Others went forth into the field
themselves. At first, most of these were missionary wives; later
single women paid by the denominational boards went out.
The single women had a harder time being accepted, because
women were not supposed to act independently of the men
in their families, but the life of the wife was arguably the
harder. The missionary's wife was expected to testify to the
"heathen" women as her husband did to the men, but at the
same time she was responsible for the care of her own household, and usually she was pregnant or nursing a baby. Sadly,
many of these children did not survive. And often the young
mother herself had a short life. The life of Ann Judson will
serve as an example that was repeated a hundred times.

Adoniram Judson, Ann's husband, was one of a group of
young men, students at Williams College in Massachusetts,
who were inspired to become Christian evangelists in foreign
lands. It is said that they made a pledge to go into the mission
field at a secret meeting in the shelter of a haystack, hence the

"Haystack Band." Two years later, in 1810, they prevailed on the Congregational Church to form the American Board of Commissioners for Foreign Missions and volunteered to be commissioned.

Some of these early enterprises were admirably ecumenical, but here we really need to be conscious of the theological conflicts between denominations. How did Judson, starting out under the auspices of the Congregational Church, become one of the heroes of the Baptist missionary movement?

Well, during the long sea voyage from Salem, Massachusetts, to Calcutta by way of the Cape of Good Hope, the Judsons engaged in Bible study and reflection, which led them to the opinion that the correct view of baptism was the Baptist position: baptism by immersion of adults rather than baptism by sprinkling of infants. On arrival in Calcutta, Adoniram and Ann were rebaptized. At once he wrote resigning his connection with the Congregational Board of Missions, inquiring if the Baptists in the United States would form a society, and offering himself as its first missionary. This was done; hence the prominence of the name "Judson" in Baptist enterprises—for example, Judson Press!

Since the Judsons are remembered so well a hundred and seventy-five years later, and since they are typical of some of the pluses and minuses of the foreign field, we will take a more detailed look at them. Wishing to marry Ann Hasseltine and take her with him to the field, Judson had written to her father in these words:

> I have now to ask whether you can consent to part with your daughter early next spring, to see her no more in this world? Whether you can consent to her departure to a heathen land, and her subjection to the hardships and sufferings of a missionary life? whether you can consent to her exposure to the dangers of the ocean; to the fatal influence of the southern climate of India; to every kind of want and distress; to degradation, insults, persecution, and perhaps a violent death? Can you consent to all this for the sake of Him who left His heavenly home and died for her and for you . . . for the sake of Zion and the glory of God?[3]

It occurs to the modern woman that he should have asked those questions of *Ann!* I guess he did, for she is quoted as saying that her decision to marry him was not based on her love for a man, but on her "obligation to God . . . with a full conviction of its being a call."[4]

Before the Judsons and another couple set sail, the Rev. Jonathan Allen preached a far-sighted sermon that is remarkable because it speaks to the women's own ministry, not just to what they could do for their husbands:

> It will be your business, my dear children, to teach these women, to whom your husbands can have but little or no access. Go then, and do all in your power, to enlighten their minds, and bring them to the knowledge of the truth. . . . Teach them to realize that they are not an inferior race of creatures; but stand upon a par with men. Teach them that they have immortal souls; and are no longer to burn themselves in the same fire with the bodies of their departed husbands. Go, bring them from their cloisters into the assemblies of the saints.[5]

This in 1812, when most white men were by no means convinced that *their* wives, sisters, and daughters were "not an inferior race of creatures!"

Ann and Adoniram did marry, they did set out for India thirteen days after their wedding, and she, as well as her husband, did suffer most of the hardships that Judson had predicted in his letter to his future father-in-law. Since we are concentrating on women in foreign missions, and since Adoniram has been justly acclaimed, let us reflect on the rest of Ann's brief life. She translated the Gospel of Matthew into Siamese; translated a catechism, the stories of Jonah and Daniel, and a tract into Burmese; and translated a Burmese sacred book into English.[6] She conducted many classes for women and girls, teaching them to read. Let us not forget that native women in these lands were often not taught at all, nor did they receive any medical treatment, unless and until these opportunities could be provided by those of their own sex. This was, of course, a powerful motivation for American women to go into the mission field; the story of Dr. Ida Scudder, whom we will consider later, will serve as a good example of this.

But Ann's greatest contribution to the cause of missions was her inspirational writing. She wrote heartrending accounts of child marriages, female infanticide, and suttee, the practice of widows being burned alive on the funeral pyres of their dead husbands. At best, married women survived in what Ann referred to as "listless idleness." What she wrote about native women served, as she hoped, to encourage many other missionary efforts, as well as increased support from the home front.

During the thirteen years she served in Burma, many of the predicted hardships came true—Adoniram's confinement for nearly two years in a dreadful Burmese prison, her own ill health, and the death of a baby son. Ann Judson died in 1826 at the age of thirty-seven.

Another bold spirit who was willing to step forth in faith and accomplish much was Sarah Doremus. Married to a wealthy New York businessman and eventually the mother of eight daughters and a son, Doremus worked tirelessly for many causes, including work in behalf of women prisoners, a women's hospital, and a home for aged women. Someone has said that the credit should go to her servants, who freed her for that work. Yes, she did have servants, money to spend, and a sympathetic husband, and we are sure she appreciated these blessings, but many rich women then and now never use their blessings to help others.

When Sarah Doremus and her friends heard David Abeel, an American missionary to China from the Reformed Church who had returned to the United States, describe the oppressed and miserable plight of Oriental women, they were moved. Abeel begged for prayers and "as many teachers as all the ladies in Christendom can send or support."[7]

Sarah Doremus and her friends formed the Women's Union Missionary Society of America in 1861, with Doremus as organizer and first president. The Society and the daughter societies that quickly sprang up in other parts of the United

States soon supported missionaries and other Christian workers in Burma, India, China, Syria, Greece, and Japan. Many of
those sent were single women, a practice that previously had
been rare. A clergyman of her acquaintance is said to have felt
that it was important for *him* to attend every meeting of the
Missionary Society because "you never can tell what these
ladies are going to pray for!" Although many Christian
churches were horrified by the idea of ordaining women, the
same feeling did not always apply to these "labors for the
benefit of the female sex," probably because the men did not
envision the women missionaries as ministering to men. At
any rate, there were now single women in the foreign field, as
well as the wives.

The very first single woman, not the widow of a missionary, sent to the foreign field was an African American woman,
Betsey Stockton, who went to Hawaii, then known as the
Sandwich Islands, in 1822. She had been born a slave in the
Stockton family and was later owned by Dr. Ashbel Green,
president of Princeton College. Betsey was given the run of
the Green library and educated herself. She was freed when
she was twenty. In Hawaii she ran a school, and after she
returned to the United States, she conducted schools for Indian children in Canada and later for African American children in Philadelphia and Princeton.[8] Like Katie Ferguson of
the Sunday school movement, her place in the history of
Christian education has been sadly undervalued.

Actually, the role of missionary women in the foreign
field in the 1800s has as a whole been sadly undervalued. Like
the contemporary picture of the temperance worker, they
have been unfairly stereotyped. Page Smith described them as
"grim, thin-lipped fanatics, putting muumuus on unself-con-
scious women and filling happy natives with Western inhibi-
tions."[9] In truth, the happy natives were more fiction than
fact. In the foreign lands to which the missionaries went,
females were victimized by child marriages (with the girl as
young as six years), bound feet, female infanticide, and concu-

binage. For many native women, missionary women were genuine deliverers.

Medicine was a specialty in which women missionaries excelled, partly because of the severely restricted role that male missionary doctors could play in the treatment of women and girls. In 1870, Dr. Clara Swain became the first woman doctor to go to India, treating as many as seven thousand patients a year. A Methodist, she considered herself primarily an evangelist and was delighted to be invited to become the palace physician for a Muslim rajah, so that in addition to treating the physical ailments of his family and servants, she could also bring the message of Christ to their lives.

Dr. Ida Scudder was brought up in a missionary household; her father and grandfather were medical missionaries to India. As a child, Ida decided that she was not going to be a missionary because the life was too hard and involved too many painful separations for the children who went back to the United States to school. But it seemed that God had other plans for her life. She told the moving story of "three knocks in the night." Three Indian men—Brahmin, Hindu, and Muslim—knocked on the door of the Scudders' house in one night, in need of medical help for their wives, who were in the throes of difficult childbirth. Ida's father would gladly have gone, but none of the men would let him touch their womenfolk. Ida recounted the story later:

> I could not sleep that night—it was too terrible. Within the very touch of my hand there were three young girls dying because no woman would help them. I spent much of the night in anguish and prayer. I did not want to spend my life in India. . . . I went to bed . . . after praying much for guidance. . . . Early in the morning . . . I sent out my servant, and he came back saying that all of them had died during the night. . . . After much thought and prayer, I went to my father and mother and told them that I must go home and study medicine, and come back to India to help such women.[10]

Although most of these women have been all but forgotten by historians, their contributions were responsible, along with male missionaries, for changing the course of history:

Colonialism in and of itself never taught a single native woman to read, founded a school or started a college or a hospital. . . . Education more than conversion was the agency of change and in this venture American women played a major role, if not *the* major role. . . . They wrote books, started printing presses and founded colleges, kindergartens, training schools, hospitals, and orphanages. . . . Their children became missionaries, doctors, politicians, and, in very considerable numbers, college professors. Yet as far as academic history is concerned, it is as if all of this had never happened. American historians have ignored this whole extraordinary episode, presumably because it happened outside the geographical limits of the United States. But if it is not part of American history, it is certainly a crucial part of world history.[11]

Notes

1. R. Pierce Beaver, *American Protestant Women in World Mission,* rev. ed. (Grand Rapids, Mich.: Wm. B. Eerdmans Publishing Co., 1980), p. 14.
2. Ruth Tucker, *Daughters of the Church: Women and Ministry from New Testament Times to the Present* (Grand Rapids, Mich.: Zondervan Publishing House, 1987), p. 66.
3. Page Smith, *Daughters of the Promised Land* (Boston: Little, Brown & Co. Inc., 1970), pp. 183–184.
4. Tucker, *Daughters of the Church,* p. 295.
5. Beaver, *American Protestant Women,* pp. 51–52.
6. Joan Jacobs Brumberg, *Mission for Life: The Story of the Family of Adoniram Judson* (New York: Free Press, a division of Macmillan Publishing Co, Inc., 1980), p. 258.
7. Beaver, *American Protestant Women,* p. 90.
8. Ibid., p. 67.
9. Smith, *Daughters of the Promised Land,* p. 184.
10. Tucker, *Daughters of the Church,* p. 320.
11. Smith, *Daughters of the Promised Land,* p. 201.

CHAPTER SEVEN

Down with Demon Rum!

To contemporary women, the temperance movement seems to have been a kind of joke. We remember Carry (yes, she did spell her name that way) Nation going into saloons wielding her little hatchet, and we picture all those grim-faced women who hated men and didn't want them to have a good time. Well, Carry *was* a little crazy, as we shall see, and some women, then as now, probably did hate men, but the whole story was very much different.

Alcoholism was a problem in the nineteenth century just as it is today. Then, as now, the consequences were medical problems for the drinker and harm to the family unit—loss of respect for the alcoholic, possible physical and/or mental abuse of the other family members, humiliation in the eyes of the community, and financial hardship. Since alcoholism was not considered a disease, there were no opportunities for treatment. At that time most alcoholics were men, since nineteenth-century culture did not permit women to drink. Of course, some women were able to hide their addiction; some were even addicted to "tonics," which contained large percentages of alcohol. For the most part, however, wives, children, and female relatives were the ones who faced the problems of living with an alcoholic. Dependent upon men for all their worldly needs, women believed that the only solution to the problems of alcoholism was to make it illegal to purchase alcohol at all. Susan B. Anthony, speaking in Chicago in 1875, said:

Compelled by their position in society to depend on men for
subsistence, for food, clothes, shelter, for every chance even to
earn a dollar, they [women] have no way of escape from the
besotted victims of appetite and passion with whom their lot is
cast. . . . No one can doubt that the sufferings of the sober,
virtuous woman, in legal subjection to the mastership of a
drunken, immoral husband and father over herself and children,
not only from physical abuse, but from spiritual shame and humiliation, must be such as the man himself can not possibly compre-
hend. . . . The roots of the giant evil, intemperance, are not
merely moral and social; they extend deep and wide into the
financial and political structure of the government; and whenever
women, or men, shall intelligently set themselves about the work
of uprooting the liquor traffic, they will find something more than
tears and prayers needful to the talk. Financial and political
power must be combined with moral and social influence, all
bound together in one earnest, energetic, persistent force.[1]

The word "temperance," of course, was not used in the
sense of moderation or self-restraint. In the 1780s, Dr. Benjamin Rush, a wise and farsighted man, really did advocate
temperance or moderation, especially the restriction of alcohol to moderate amounts of wine or beer. His popular essay
"Inquiry into the Effects of Ardent Spirits" inspired the
founding of the first United States temperance society in
1808. But what most "Daughters of Temperance" meant was
total abstinence, and they often resorted to extreme mea-
sures, such as pouring barrels of whiskey out into the gutters,
to achieve their goals.

More, perhaps, than any of the other reform movements
of the day, the cause was taken up by Christian women. Temperance, unlike some of the other women's causes, had the
backing of the local churches. Many Protestant churches even
began serving grape juice instead of wine in the Communion
service, saying that a person who was trying *not* to drink might
be overcome by the small taste of wine received at the Lord's
Table and go on to consume alcohol in other forms and in
greater quantities. Interestingly, the idea of complete abstinence as the only cure for alcoholism is now the principle of
Alcoholics Anonymous.

As mentioned before, the vast majority of problem drinkers were men. The vast majority of temperance society workers were women; not all however—the Eighteenth Amendment, after all, was passed before the Nineteenth. This means that, as only men could vote in national elections, prohibition was voted into law by men.

It is fascinating to note the degree to which a sort of interlocking directorate of Christian women appears in the history of all these movements—abolition, temperance, and the various aspects of women's rights. Susan B. Anthony, usually associated with the women's suffrage movement, for instance, was president of the Rochester, New York, Daughters of Temperance, and went as a delegate to many temperance conventions. There she met other activists, such as Amelia Bloomer, the editor of a temperance newspaper, *The Lily.* Bloomer, however, is most often remembered in connection with dress reform for women.

By 1855 thirteen states had passed their own prohibition laws, but the tide receded and a number of those states repealed the laws. After the Civil War, interest in the temperance movement again heightened. The Woman's Christian Temperance Union (WCTU), eventually to have a membership in the hundreds of thousands, was organized in Ohio, in 1865. Page Smith, in *Daughters of the Promised Land,* says of the WCTU:

> The passion that had ignited the abolitionist movement and the crusade for woman's rights flared up once more, drawing together new legions of Christian ladies. The fight was, in part, directed against a genuine evil, almost endemic drunkenness, and in part against the image of the male—rough, sodden, bestial, and above all, disappointing—that had a strong appeal to so many nineteenth-century wives.[2]

Most temperance writers and speakers referred to drunkenness as the cause of crime. One may say that drunkenness and crime are not necessarily inseparable, but present statistics bear out the claim that violence is often the corollary of substance abuse, whether it be addiction to heroin or to alcohol, and we must suppose that it has always been true.

Now for Carry Nation. Just as we shall see that the Claflin sisters must have been thorns in the side of the moderate elements of the suffrage movement, Carry Nation must sometimes have been an embarrassment to the temperance workers. One cannot imagine a personality more different from the dignified Frances Willard, President of the WCTU.

Carry had been married briefly to an alcoholic, Charles Gloyd, and the experience left her with a burning hatred for liquor and saloons. Having in the meantime divorced Gloyd and married David Nation, she came up with the theory that since saloons in Kansas, a "dry" state, were in violation of the law, they were outside the protection of the law and thus were fair game for destruction with the hatchet that she carried with her. "Alone or with a few hymn-singing supporters, she invaded 'joints,' castigated the 'rummies' present, and concluded with a highly destructive 'hatchetation' of the property."[3] Among the sites of her visits were the barroom of the Hotel Carey in Wichita and the saloon of the Kansas state senate. One must admit that a saloon in the senate building of a dry state does seem like blatantly flouting the law!

In 1901, Carry's husband divorced her for desertion. She was often arrested for disturbing the peace; she paid her numerous fines by the sale of souvenir hatchets. She sometimes appeared in vaudeville at Coney Island, and briefly in 1903 in a staged adaptation of *Ten Nights in a Barroom* entitled *Hatchetation(!)* More conventional reformers, understandably, preferred not to hear about Carry.

There were close links between the causes of woman suffrage and temperance, and many women spoke in public in favor of both causes. Anna Howard Shaw, for instance, was a temperance speaker who played an important role in the battle for women's ordination, and we shall see her again in the story of the suffrage amendment. In her autobiographical *Story of a Pioneer,* she told of a not uncommon display of violent opposition to the WCTU. The temperance meeting at which she was to speak was held in Michigan in the town skating rink, and the wooden structure was filled to capacity and more. As Shaw spoke, a man dropped through a trapdoor in the ceiling and shouted, "Fire!" The building had indeed been set on fire, and Shaw directed the evacuation of the crowd, who sang hymns as they moved out in an orderly fashion. When everyone was safely outside, and the building was in flames, a local minister invited the crowd to his church. Shaw pointed out "the character of the interests we were fighting,"[4] and won many new supporters to the cause of temperance.

Today, when many people think of the Woman's Christian Temperance Union, they envision women who were concerned about no more important issues than whether or not it was wrong to put a little rum in the Christmas fruit cake. But the truth is far different. The person who had the most influence on the WCTU was, beyond a doubt, Frances Willard. When it was organized, the Union was, in the minds of most of its members, conservative and antisuffrage. But Frances Willard was elected corresponding secretary, and she had other ideas. Coming out openly for woman suffrage, she had gained enough support by 1879 to be elected national president of the WCTU. Able to project her voice to the farthest corners of a large auditorium, she was a magnificent speaker and a real showperson. Under her leadership, WCTU meetings became dramatic and colorful, with banners, martial music, and rousing oratory.

Willard knew her constituency. She portrayed voting rights as the weapon of the woman to protect the sanctity of the home and the moral purity of the nation. The slogan she coined was "For God and Home and Native Land." Another motto was "Woman will bless and brighten every place she enters, and she will enter every place." Interestingly, Willard used the phrase "like a prairie fire" to describe her cause! A large and enthusiastic membership enlisted in the cause, not only of temperance, but of a wide variety of social reforms. Page Smith tells us:

> It [WCTU] campaigned for kindergartens, police matrons, "social purity," and child labor laws, and prided itself upon its catholicity in bringing "upon one platform" Jew, Catholic, Methodist,

Universalist, Unitarian and Baptist joined in "the one pulse, a
protected home and a redeemed America." There was a measure
of truth in its claim that it "has developed the brain of woman as
no schooling ever did before, has broadened the sympathy of her
heart until it takes in all humanity, has educated her will until it
has become a mighty power, and has exalted to supreme heights
her faith in God."[5]

One example, described in Ruth Bordin's *Woman and
Temperance: The Quest for Power and Liberty,* illustrates vividly
how power and liberty for women went along with the aims
of the WCTU. In 1880, just four years after its organization,
the Michigan WCTU was the "sole instigator and major im-
plementer"[6] of the founding of a girls' reformatory. The
Michigan Union collected over twenty thousand signatures
on a petition, proposed a bill before the legislature, and succeeded in bringing about a state-supported house of shelter
for delinquent girls. What is more, the bill, as adopted, stipulated that women be appointed to a majority of places on the
institution's board of directors, the first women in Michigan
to hold public office. It also stipulated that women staff the
reformatory. When it opened, the superintendent, the physician, the teachers, and the housekeepers were all women. The
only exception was a man who ran the heating plant!

Along with the Salvation Army and the Young Women's
Christian Association (both of which, incidentally, are much
more flourishing today than the WCTU), the Union became
involved with problems that still face the urban working
woman—skills training, employment opportunities, decent
affordable housing, child care, and budgeting. Other issues
the WCTU tackled were the rescue of abandoned and delinquent children, research into the causes of alcoholism, the
establishment of hospitals to care for chronic alcoholics, and
help for their families. The organization was enlightened,
well-organized, and effective. All these facets of the WCTU
are described in a good overview of the whole temperance
movement by Ruth Bordin in *Woman and Temperance: The Quest
for Power and Liberty, 1873–1900.*

The temperance movement, like the abolition movement, encouraged women who had never before spoken in public to speak out, to be organized and efficient, and to meet other women who saw their Christianity as a call to action as well as a private matter of the soul. Once again the broom was being used for more extensive tasks than sweeping the hearth. As the group became involved in efforts to reform society in all these ways, it became increasingly clear to even the most traditional members that they were never going to get anywhere without the vote. Thus, the temperance movement and the suffrage movement, which had been existing separately for years, became intertwined. Whether this was fortunate or unfortunate for the cause of suffrage is not really clear, as we shall see in the chapter about voting rights.

Notes

1. Aileen Kraditor, *Up from the Pedestal* (New York: New York Times Books, 1968), pp. 159–160.
2. Page Smith, *Daughters of the Promised Land* (Boston: Little, Brown & Co., Inc., 1970), p. 255.
3. Robert McHenry, *Famous American Women: A Biographical Dictionary from Colonial Times to the Present* (Mineola, N.Y.: Dover Publications Inc., 1983), p. 299.
4. Anna Howard Shaw, *Story of a Pioneer* (Millwood, N.Y.: Kraus Reprint & Periodicals, repr. of 1915 ed.), p. 171.
5. Smith, *Daughters of the Promised Land,* p. 256.
6. Ruth Bordin, *Women and Temperance: The Quest for Power and Liberty, 1873–1900* (New Brunswick, N.J.: Rutgers University Press, 1990), p. xiii.

CHAPTER EIGHT

It's a Man's World Until Women Vote!

Why was the struggle for votes for women so overwhelmingly important? As Eleanor Flexner points out in the introduction to *Century of Struggle:*

> Full political citizenship was, for women as for any other group arbitrarily deprived of it, a vital step toward winning full human dignity and the recognition that women, too, are endowed with the faculty of reason, the power of judgment, the capacity for social responsibility and effective action.[1]

As women, and particularly Christian women, became more and more active in such causes as abolition, temperance, prison reform, hospital reform, and women's rights to own property and control their earnings, it became increasingly clear to most of them that the best way to attain these longed-for goals was to work for the vote. Remember, the vote was one of the things regarded as an inalienable right by the Seneca Falls Women's Rights convention in 1848, but fifty years later, woman suffrage seemed as far away as ever.

The term, incidentally, preferred by women who worked for the vote was "suffragist," not "suffragette." The latter was originally demeaning, much like the word "libber" today. No advocate of women's liberation would call herself a "libber," and likewise most advocates of votes for women cringed when referred to as "suffragettes."

The story of the position of the Woman's Christian Temperance Union illustrates the way in which the minds of many women changed over time on the suffrage issue. Among the many causes for which the WCTU worked were reforms of the prison, the jail, and the juvenile asylum. For instance, WCTU insisted on the presence of a female warden or police matron when women offenders were in jail, and the appointment of women to boards of trustees of institutions caring for dependent or delinquent children. As all these reforms involved changes in existing law, Frances Willard argued:

> When women come to consciousness they must inevitably ask questions like these: Why should we have no voice in making the laws under which we may be imprisoned or executed? Why should women have no hand in pleading woman's cause or determining her penalties? Why should men, and men alone, have the power of life and death over women?[2]

The WCTU, with its thousands of members, thus became a strong influence in the suffrage movement. This had both fortunate and unfortunate aspects, because votes for women and prohibition laws became bound up together in the perception of many people, including the producers and distributors of alcoholic beverages. For example, a suffrage constitutional amendment in California was defeated in 1896 largely by the efforts of the Liquor Dealers' League. They met in San Francisco and sent a letter to saloon keepers, hotel proprietors, druggists, and grocers throughout the state, saying in part, "It is to your interest and ours to vote against this amendment. We request and urge you to vote and work against it and do all you can to defeat it. See your neighbor in the same line of business as yourself, and have him be with you in this matter."[3] Thus, woman suffrage was opposed by the unlikely union of (a) very conservative people who thought women were too pure and dainty for the rough world of politics and (b) saloon keepers who saw votes for women as dangerous to their business interests. And the saloon keepers had the advantage of having a lot of money to pour into the campaign! No wonder the California amendment lost.

Susan B. Anthony, who had unusually good sense about such matters, saw that the coalition of prohibition and suffrage had some drawbacks for the suffrage movement. To the president of the California WCTU, Anthony wrote:

> There are many excellent men in California who are not total abstainers, but who believe in wine as the people of Italy and France believe in it; and I think that, in waging our [suffrage] campaign, we should be careful not to run against the prejudices or the pecuniary interests of that class. . . . We should be extremely careful to base all our arguments upon the right of every individual to have his or her opinion counted at the ballot-box, whether it is in accordance with ours or not. Therefore, the amendment must not be urged as a measure for temperance, social purity, or any other reform, but simply as a measure to give to women the right to vote yea or nay on each and all of them.[4]

Horace Greeley of the New York *Tribune,* who had supported women in most of their struggles, tried to get Susan B. Anthony to stop campaigning for woman suffrage after the Civil War because, he told her, this was the Negro's hour. But she was not willing to wait. He said to her, "Miss Anthony, you know the bullet and the ballot go together. If you vote, are you ready to fight?" "Yes, Mr. Greeley," Anthony retorted, "just as you fought in the late war—at the point of a goose quill!"[5]

This problem—whether or not women should step back and let African American men have their turn first—was one of the causes of the split in the ranks between the American Woman Suffrage Association and the National Woman Suffrage Association. Another problem was that Anthony and others thought that voting rights were so closely tied to other civil rights that members should be allowed to campaign for such "dangerous" topics as a single, rather than a double, standard of morality. This stance led inevitably to the participation of sensational characters such as Victoria Claflin Woodhull, who ran for president of the United States in 1872.

Victoria was one of the most remarkable figures in the suffrage movement. Her personal idiosyncracies, like Carry Nation's, did much to make her participation in any movement more of a handicap than an asset. Victoria and her sister Tennessee, the fifth and the last of ten children in a family at

odds with prevailing standards of respectability, supported
the whole family by conducting seances and inducing "mirac-
ulous" cures. Married at fifteen to Dr. Canning Woodhull,
Victoria divorced him, partly because of Dr. Woodhull's
drinking, and later married Colonel James Blood, who had
abandoned his wife and family to go through the Ozarks with
Victoria in a covered wagon, performing feats of psychic healing and predicting the future. Here she heard a voice telling
her to go to a certain address in New York City. "Who are
you?" she asked, and the vision spelled out the name "Demosthenes." Victoria, Tennessee, Blood, and Victoria's two
children, Byron and Zulu Maude, went to New York and
found the house just as the spirit had predicted, and on the
parlor table, a book entitled *The Orations of Demosthenes*.

In New York, the Claflin sisters became a force to reckon
with. They advised people on the stock market, pointed out
political graft, urged world government, and began a magazine, *Woodhull and Claflin's Weekly*. The journal printed the first
English translation of Marx's *Communist Manifesto* and promoted birth control and free love. Demosthenes had told her,
among other things, that she was to be president of the United
States. A new Equal Rights Party nominated her, with Frederick Douglass for vice president. Douglass had known nothing
about the nomination, and declined it. Understandably, the
whole episode had unfortunate effects on the perception of
the kind of woman who would work for the cause of suffrage.

Susan B. Anthony is now considered one of the most
influential workers for woman's vote, but even she had her
critics. Partly because of her accepting attitude toward rebels
such as the Claflin sisters, Quaker Anthony was criticized all
her life by those who thought she was not a Christian. Once,
a delegate to a WCTU convention told the members that she
did not want Frances Willard as president because she had
insulted them by inviting to the platform Anthony, who "did
not recognize God." "Well," another delegate replied, "I
don't know about that, but I do know that God has recognized
her and her work for the last thirty years."[6] On another occa-

sion, Anthony was interviewed for the New York *World* by the celebrated newspaperwoman Nellie Bly, who asked her, "Do you pray?" Her answer: "I pray every single second of my life; not on my knees, but with my work. My prayer is to lift woman to equality with man. Work and worship are one with me."[7]

Anthony's good friend, Dr. Anna Howard Shaw, told this story:

> Once we went to a particularly orthodox town to hold a convention. As the suffragists had been called all sorts of opprobrious names, infidel among them, we decided to try to impress the people that we were not all those things that we had been called. So Miss Anthony introduced me as "a regular ordained minister, and my right bower." The audience laughed. Later, Miss Anthony asked me why they laughed at her introduction. When I told her that she had called me her right bower, she looked puzzled, and said, "Well, you are my right hand man. Isn't that being a right bower?" And then this orthodox minister had to tell the Quaker friend what a *right bower* was.[8] [For those who are not familiar with the card game of euchre, the right bower is the jack of the trump suit, and the highest card in the deck. And many in the audience considered card playing wicked!]

The two suffrage organizations—American Woman Suffrage Association and National Woman Suffrage Association—existed side by side from 1869 to 1890. Voting rights were at first gained state by state or territory by territory. (A good summary of this is in Flexner, Chapters 12 and 16.)

There were, of course, women who worked *against* woman suffrage, such as Mrs. Arthur Dodge, chairwoman of the antisuffragist movement, and her tireless assistant, Mrs. Annie Nathan Meyers. As William Chute tells us:

> Mrs. Meyers had been a leader in the fight for the improvement of educational opportunities for women and, in 1889, was one of the founders of Barnard College, the female adjunct of Columbia University. What could seem more obvious than that she should be equally as enthusiastic in the battle to give women the ballot? Over the years, however, this educationalist became so disgusted with the extravagant promises for making the world moral and pure by this single process, that she refused her support. . . .[9]

One has to admit, however reluctantly, that Meyers had a point. It was no doubt a mistake to argue, as many women did, that votes for women would mean the end of war, immorality, crime in the streets, and unfair labor practices in the marketplace. Like the political party that campaigns that it will, if elected, balance the budget, increase support for worthy causes, and cut taxes, the promises are obviously impossible to fulfill. This did not mean, however, that universal suffrage was a mistake, just that it was not a panacea for all the ills of society.

By 1912 women had the vote in Wyoming, Colorado, Utah, Idaho, Washington, California, Oregon, Kansas, and Arizona. But the battle for *national* woman suffrage was just beginning. Women were told that if President Wilson wanted the suffrage amendment, it would be voted on in Washington. Alice Paul, a Quaker like Susan B. Anthony, headed up the nonviolent protest. In 1917 suffragists, carrying banners of purple, white, and gold, began picketing the White House. Many of the banners were inscribed with Wilson's own words—for example: "The time has come to conquer or submit. For us there can be but one choice. We have made it."

Sixteen women picketed the White House on Bastille Day, 1917, with banners reading "Liberty, Equality and Fraternity." Arrested, like hundreds of other suffragists, for "obstructing traffic," they were sentenced to sixty days in the Occoquan Workhouse. The conditions of their imprisonment are horrifying to read about. Among other indignities, they were served food in which worms were floating. After their release, the women had sixteen silver pins made up, each a replica of a prison door with a tiny chain and small peephole, representing an opening through which food was passed. They wore the pins to remind them of what they had been through. But in spite of this treatment, they did not give up. For a year and a half, the picketing went on. At last, the amendment came to a vote.

The Nineteenth or "Susan B. Anthony" Amendment finally passed the House on January 10, 1918. The vote was 274 to 136, exactly the two-thirds majority needed. In June of 1919, the Senate approved the Anthony Amendment. Then, of course, it had to go to the states for ratification. Thirty-six states had to ratify the amendment. The final critical vote took place on August 18, 1920, in Tennessee. Opponents wore red roses, while supporters wore the purple, gold, and white ribbons of the suffrage cause. Tennessee's legislature passed the amendment, and eight days later the Nineteenth Amendment to the Constitution became the law of the land.

Supporters believed that they had enough votes to carry the Tennessee legislature, "but when the amendment came up for action, railroad, liquor, and business interests plied the legislators with so much liquor [this during Prohibition!] that a number of members wavered and reduced the women's margin to a tie. After unbearable suspense, the tie was broken by a man [Harry Burn, the youngest member of the House] who confessed that he was changing his vote because his mother wished him to support ratification."[10] The American woman was at last given the right to vote; the Nineteenth Amendment became law on August 26, 1920, in time for women to vote in the presidential election of that year.

Notes

1. Eleanor Flexner, *Century of Struggle: The Woman's Rights Movement in the United States* (Cambridge, Mass.: Harvard University Press, 1975), p. xii.
2. Sheila Rothman, *Woman's Proper Place* (New York: Basic Books Inc., Publishers-Harper & Row, Publishers, Inc., 1978), p. 69.
3. Ida Husted Harper, *The Life and Work of Susan B. Anthony, vol. 2*, 1899, quoted by Flexner in *Century of Struggle*, p. 224.
4. Ibid, p. 882.
5. Elizabeth Anticaglia, *Twelve American Women* (Chicago: Nelson-Hall Publishers, 1975), p. 85.
6. Nanette Paul, *The Great Woman Statesman* (New York: Hogan-Paulus Corporation, 1925), p. 93.
7. Ibid., p. 143.
8. Ibid., pp. 154–155.
9. William J. Chute, *The American Scene: 1860 to the Present* (New York: Bantam Books-Bantam Doubleday Dell Publishing Group Inc., 1965), p. 265.
10. Caroline Bird, *Born Female* (New York: Pocket Books-Simon & Schuster Inc., 1969), pp. 29–30.

CHAPTER NINE

Emancipation from the Crinoline

Women's dress seems like a comparatively minor matter compared to rights to the ballot, higher education, ordination, family planning, and the like; but, if we think back to what women's attire was like in the nineteenth century, we begin to see that dress reform was important. So long as the women were tightly corseted and clothed in layer upon layer of long heavy petticoats and skirts, their freedom to move about and even to breathe easily was greatly hampered.

Since long skirts were obviously one of the problems, the solution seemed to be the comparative freedom of some form of long trousers for women. Many of those who opposed this form of dress quoted Scripture to the effect that: "The woman shall not wear that which pertaineth unto a man, neither shall a man put on a woman's garment; for all that do so *are* abomination unto the LORD thy God" (Deuteronomy 22:5, KJV). This seems clear indeed, but how about the twelfth verse of that chapter? It reads, "Thou shalt make thee fringes upon the four quarters of thy vesture, wherewith thou coverest *thyself.*" This applies to garments, too. Why was verse 5 binding in the 1800s in America, while verse 12 was not? As usual, Bible interpretation was carried on by the male clergy, and only the verses they wanted to use were considered.

Elizabeth Smith Miller (1822–1911), a relative of Elizabeth Cady Stanton, was the designer of the "bloomer" costume made famous by Mrs. Amelia Bloomer, who wrote about it in her abolition paper, *The Lily*. It was a "short" skirt—short in comparison to the floor-sweeping costumes of the day—under which were worn "Turkish" trousers or pantaloons. When Stanton saw Miller going up the stairs carrying a baby and a lighted lamp, and not having to hold up her long, heavy skirts, she was converted to the new form of dress. Before long, however, most of its advocates abandoned the bloomer costume because of the unbearable persecution undergone by its wearers when they went out in public. Often they were followed down the street by small boys chanting rude jingles or were ostracized at public gatherings. Stanton wrote to Anthony in 1854, "We put the dress on for greater freedom, but what is physical freedom compared with mental bondage? . . . It is not wise, Susan, to use up so much energy and feeling that way. You can put them to better use. I speak from experience."[1]

Being uncomfortable and inconvenienced were not the only problems caused by the fashions. The enormous number of hand-hemmed ruffles made dressmaking time-consuming and hard on the eyesight. The dresses were also difficult to keep clean and pressed. Thorstein Veblen, in his well-known *Theory of the Leisure Class,* pointed out that women's dress was a prime example of "conspicuous consumption." In other words, women dressed in that manner, not because it was convenient or becoming, but because a dress advertised to others that the woman (or her father or husband) could afford all those yards of fabric. Thus, the addition of one dress to a woman's wardrobe could mean the spending of a large quantity of money and time.

The most serious problem with women's fashions in the nineteenth century was the effect that they had on women's health. The "wasp waist," along with the boned corsets that made it possible, was so confining as to make breathing difficult. When exercise, such as riding a bicycle, was recommended as healthful, there were those who objected on the grounds that a woman's constitution would not permit such violent exertion. It was well known, they said, that women and girls were subject to fainting spells if they exercised. The truth was that the manner in which their waists and bosoms were confined in "stays" caused their shortness of breath.

Catherine Beecher, sister of Harriet Beecher Stowe, "became so obsessed with the question of the health of American women that she spent forty years trying to discover why chronic illness was the lot of 'the women of this generation.' "[2] She found that many women were "delicate" or "habitual invalids." After a great deal of research, inspired in part by her own ill health, she came to the conclusion that the problem lay in the clothes women wore, their confinement to poorly ventilated houses, and their lack of exercise and fresh air. As a result, she became one of the first active advocates of physical education for women, which she introduced in the 1850s into the course of study at the Hartford Female Seminary in Hartford, Connecticut. Of course, along with the fresh air and exercise would have to go the abandonment of the tight stays and long heavy petticoats. She preached the doctrine of "Light, Air, Sleep, Food and Clothing."[3]

The magazine *The Revolution* pointed out another connection between women's lack of opportunities to improve their lot and the clothing they had to wear:

> Working women . . . dress yourselves in costume, like daughters of the regiment, and be conductors in our cars and railroads, drive hacks. If your petticoats stand in the way of bread, virtue and freedom, cut them off. . . . Woman's dress keeps her out of a multitude of employments where she could make good wages. We heard of a family of daughters out West who, being left suddenly to depend on themselves, decided to ignore all woman's work at low wages, so they donned male attire. One went to work in a lumber yard, one on a steamboat, one drove a hack in a Western city, and in a few years with economy they laid up enough to buy a handsome farm where they now live in comfort.[4]

Tennessee Claflin, the younger sister of Victoria Claflin Woodhull, was one of the proponents of more liberating dress for women. Like Woodhull's advocacy of votes for women and Carry Nation's advocacy of temperance, Tennessee's stand may have done the cause more harm than good, but it is interesting to see what she said about dress in 1871:

> One of the first principles of dress, regarding health, is *that all portions of the body should be evenly covered,* so that there shall always be a free and uninfluenced circulation of blood. . . . It is a well known fact, that since the present fashions of padding and bustle-wearing came in vogue, the class of complaints known as Female Weakness have increased a hundred fold. . . . It is time . . . to be honest enough to speak the truth about these things, which are fettering and diseasing women and producing a generation of sickly children.[5]

It was not until the '20s, at about the time when women received voting privileges, that dress was really reformed very much. The "boyish bob" freed women from the burden of masses of elaborately dressed hair. Dresses became shorter, straight, and relatively uncomplicated by frills and furbelows. This should have made them cheaper, but, unfortunately, clothing has continued to be a prime example of conspicuous consumption.

Bathing suits came to be short enough so that the wearer could actually swim, not just paddle about in the water. The magazine *The Revolution* promoted the idea of women working at jobs in which petticoats would get in the way; the dream came true, and soon slacks could be worn in public. Eventually hats and gloves were no longer required attire for women when they went outdoors. The result has been emancipation indeed. When women of all classes of society were given the opportunity to dress sensibly, they began to live longer and healthier lives, and they began to have more opportunities available for work and recreation.

Notes

1. Eleanor Flexner, *Century of Struggle: The Women's Rights Movement in the United States* (Cambridge, Mass.: Harvard University Press, 1975), p. 84.
2. Page Smith, *Daughters of the Promised Land* (Boston: Little, Brown & Co., Inc., 1970), p. 133.
3. Ibid.
4. Judith Papachristou, *Women Together: A History in Documents of the Women's Movement in the United States* (New York: Alfred Knopf, 1976), p. 61.
5. Aileen Kraditor, editor, *Up from the Pedestal* (New York: New York Times Books, 1968), p. 131.

CHAPTER TEN

The Dangerous Experiment

We in the United States are so used to the concept of universal education, at least up to the middle teen years, that it is hard to realize that at one time it was considered dangerous to society to teach the lower classes to read and write. They might get ideas above their station, and then where would the servants and unskilled laborers come from? But as democracy as an ideal came to be more widely accepted, schooling was provided for boys, even boys from poor families, to enable them to read, write, and do simple arithmetic.

The next question was whether to include girls in this "common" schooling. As early as the days of the American Revolution, there were voices crying out for the education of girls. Even before the publication in England of Mary Wollstonecraft's *Vindication of the Rights of Women,* usually considered to be the opening gun in the battle for women's rights, Judith Sargent Murray wrote on the subject of women's education. She was the daughter of a delegate to the Massachusetts convention that ratified the Constitution. Using the name of Constantia, Murray wrote for *Massachusetts Magazine.* In an article published in 1790, reflecting on the disparity of educational opportunities open to boys and girls, she wrote:

> Should it still be vociferated, "Your domestic employments are sufficient"—I would calmly ask, is it reasonable, that a candidate for immortality, for the joys of heaven, an intelligent being, who is to spend an eternity in contemplating the works of Deity,

should at present be so degraded, as to be allowed no other ideas, than those which are suggested by the mechanism of a pudding, or the sewing of the seams of a garment?[1]

Like the women at Seneca Falls a half century later, Murray saw the connection between woman's role as a citizen of the kingdom of God and her role as a citizen of the new United States.

In a letter to her husband, written in 1776, Abigail Adams said,

> If you complain of neglect of Education in sons, What [sic] shall I say with regard to daughters, who every day experience the want of it. With regard to the Education of my own children I find myself soon out of my depth, and destitute and deficient in every part of Education. . . . If we mean to have Heroes, Statesmen and Philosophers, we should have learned women.[2]

Today's women, of course, would have preferred that Abigail pleaded for women to be educated for their own careers as stateswomen and philosophers, but for her day, over two hundred years ago, she was at least far-sighted to have seen the need for women to be educated as mothers!

Dr. Benjamin Rush, active as well in the temperance movement, was one of those who spoke out for a new system of education for young women. Among the subjects that Dr. Rush felt the state of society required of women were the English language and writing; geography; the reading of books of history, biography and travel, as an antidote to the alarming increase in the popularity of the novel; vocal music, as an aid to strengthening the body; dancing, which he considered by no means improper; and religious instruction.[3]

Inevitably, as girls were introduced to subjects such as history and geography, they began to think of going on, as their brothers did, to higher education, at least to what we would now call high school—the female seminary. One of the earliest publications on this subject was Hannah Crocker's "Observations on the Real Rights of Women," published in 1818. She rejected the current idea that women were inherently inferior. The supporters of this idea pointed to the story of the Fall of Eve in the Garden of Eden, saying that all women inherited Eve's inferiority and therefore could not and should not aspire to education beyond the three R's. Crocker said:

> We shall consider woman restored to her original right and dignity at the commencement of the Christian dispensation; although there must be allowed some moral and physical distinction of the sexes agreeably to the order of nature, still the sentiment must predominate that the powers of the mind are equal in the sexes. . . . There can be no doubt but there is as much difference in the powers of each individual of the male sex as there is of the female; and if they received the same mode of education, their improvement would be fully equal.[4]

Emma Willard followed Crocker's lead by establishing the Troy Female Seminary; in 1821 it opened its doors as the first endowed institution for the education of girls. Shockingly, one of the courses she introduced was the study of the anatomy of the human body. The illustrations in the textbook were so dismaying to the girls' mothers that they insisted that heavy paper be pasted over them. However, the girls *were* learning algebra and geometry, geography and history and loving it!

The next step in the progress of education for girls was the establishment of Mount Holyoke, opened in 1837 as a "female seminary." It did not become a college until 1893, after Vassar, Wellesley, Smith, and Bryn Mawr; but its founder, Mary Lyons, may be said to have opened the way for them all. Mount Holyoke accepted no girl younger than sixteen, and these girls had to pass entrance examinations in subjects such as arithmetic and English grammar. Passing these exams allowed the young students to proceed to such studies as botany, chemistry, astronomy, and French. Young women had at last gone beyond the mechanics of a pudding and the sewing of a fine seam, and they were none the worse for it. There was no telling where it would lead!

Well, where it led was logically the admission of women to the first coeducational college. Lucy Stone described this event in a speech given at a national women's rights convention in Cincinnati in October, 1855:

When, with my brothers, I reached forth after the sources of
knowledge, I was reproved with, "It isn't fit for you; it doesn't
belong to women." Then there was but one college in the world
where women were admitted, and that was in Brazil. I would have
found my way there, but by the time I was prepared to go, one
was opened in the young State of Ohio—the first in the United
States where women and Negroes could enjoy opportunities with
white men.[5] [Author's note: I haven't been able to find out anything about that college in Brazil!]

The college was, of course, Oberlin, opening its doors in
Ohio to women in 1833. For four years, only the secondary
and preparatory departments were open to women, so as to
make up for the girls' previously inferior education. This was
not just prejudice against women; it was a fact that women
were not prepared, in the same way that some schools for
African American students had not prepared them adequately
for college. When, in 1837, the "college course" was opened
to women, four entered. The following year, 25 percent of the
300 students in the college course were women! College for
women was the proverbial idea whose time had come.

Lucy Stone went on to say, "In education, in marriage,
in religion, in everything, disappointment is the lot of woman.
It shall be the business of my life to deepen this disappointment in every woman's heart until she bows down to it
no longer." She might be called the Betty Friedan of her
day!

Oberlin was not, in fact, a paradise for women even after
they were admitted to its halls.

Oberlin's attitude was that women's high calling was to be the
mothers of the race, and that they should stay within that special
sphere in order that future generations should not suffer from the
want of devoted and undistracted mother care. If women became
lawyers, ministers, physicians, lecturers, politicians or any sort of
"public character" the home would suffer from neglect. . . . Washing the men's clothes, caring for their rooms, serving them at
table, listening to their orations, but themselves remaining re-
spectfully silent in public assemblages, the Oberlin "co-eds" were
being prepared for intelligent motherhood and properly subservient wifehood.[6]

Stone, of course, did not consider this concept of woman's role ideal. She refused to write the commencement address for her graduating class, as she was entitled to do because of her excellent record, because it would have had to be read aloud by a male student, as was true until 1874.

One of the main arguments against higher education for women was the supposedly bad effect of education on women's health. Dr. Edward H. Clarke wrote *Sex in Education, or a Fair Chance for the Girls.* The title actually sounds as if he was in favor of education for women. In fact, the book, which was published in 1873, expressed an almost pathological fear of what would happen if women engaged in such unnatural endeavors as studying. He spoke of "numberless pale, weak, neuralgic, dyspeptic, hysterical, menorraghic, dysmenorrheic girls and women,"[7] who had graduated from colleges only to be lifelong invalids. The probable explanation of these illnesses is discussed by Gail Griffin:

> The truly sad aspect of reading Clarke's case histories through modern eyes is how often he describes symptoms of depression which recent scholarship on women's psychology clearly explains. Often his patients seem to have fallen into depression after graduation—a simple enough phenomenon to diagnose even from a lay person's point of view when one considers the frustration and futility these women must have faced upon completing their educations only to find themselves without work to do, facing a future enclosed in the female sphere.[8]

Clarke, himself, had to drop out of medical school for a time because of an attack of hemorrhage from the lungs, but he apparently did not think his illness was related to his studies. His book went into seventeen printings; it must have been extremely influential in discouraging families from sending their girls to college. Once again, we note, God was brought into the equation; Clarke said: "Let her whole education and life be guided by the *divine* requirements of her system" (emphasis mine). Christian feminists, of course, were arguing from Scripture, as Judith Sargent Murray had done, that God wants women educated so as to carry out the divine will in their lives.

Vassar, which opened in 1865 as the first women's college with equipment and resources equal to men's colleges of the day, conducted a survey of graduates twenty years later which proved that its graduates were healthy, as were their children.[9] Maria Mitchell, professor of astronomy at Vassar, was a mild-mannered Quaker. She was the first woman admitted to the American Academy of Arts and Sciences, and later the first woman elected to the Association for the Advancement of Science.

At about the same time, women were applying for admission to the University of Michigan. In 1858 twelve women applied to the Board of Regents, who regarded the step as so momentous that they referred to it as a "dangerous experiment." Dangerous for the women or for the university? Anyway, the first woman, Madelon Stockwell, entered the University of Michigan in February 1870, and by the fall of that year thirty-four more were enrolled, eighteen of them in the department of medicine. As with Oberlin, it seems that the gates were barely open before a great throng of women and girls appeared, and not just to enroll in the easy courses of study. Other state universities open to women about this time were Iowa, Wisconsin, Kansas, Indiana, Minnesota, Missouri, and California. Perhaps in states settled by pioneer families women had already proved that they were physically and emotionally capable to face the rigors of education.

One of the last endeavors of Susan B. Anthony, in a life full of endeavors, was to get women admitted to the University of Rochester. In 1898 the board of trustees of the university announced that if a hundred thousand dollars could be raised within a year, they would make facilities for the admission of women students available. This proved impossible, but one more year's time was granted, and the sum was reduced to fifty thousand dollars. In September 1900, Anthony returned from a strenuous suffrage campaign in Wyoming to find out that the Rochester project still lacked eight thousand dollars which probably could not be raised in time. With her typical determination she raised the money, and women were admitted to the university.

With college educations available, women began to seek positions in many fields previously closed to them: medicine, law, the pulpit, astronomy, economics. Although some of these "career" women were married, marriage was no longer the only option open—this concept alone was enormously liberating. As John Raymond, the first president of Vassar, said, "Marriage is honorable in all—in man and woman both—but it is absolutely necessary to neither. . . . The suggestion [that it is necessary] is an insult alike to woman and to God."[10]

Notes

1. Eleanor Flexner, *Century of Struggle: The Women's Rights Movement in the United States* (Cambridge, Mass.: Harvard University Press, 1975), p. 16.
2. Barbara Miller Solomon, *In the Company of Educated Women: A History of Women and Higher Education in America* (New Haven, Conn.: Yale University Press, 1985), p. 1.
3. Flexner, *Century of Struggle,* p. 17.
4. Ibid., p. 25.
5. Aileen Kraditor, *Up from the Pedestal* (New York: New York Times Books, 1975), p. 71.
6. Gail Griffin, *et al, Emancipated Spirits* (privately printed, 1983), p. 12.
7. Ibid., p. 21.
8. Ibid.
9. Sheila Rothman, *Woman's Proper Place* (New York: Basic Books Inc., Publishers-Harper & Row, Publishers Inc., 1978), p. 33.
10. Ibid. p. 38.

CHAPTER ELEVEN

Your Daughters Shall Prophesy

Such burning issues as votes or higher education for women no longer seem extremely controversial today, now that they are widely accepted, but the opportunity to be ordained into the ministry, which was also a concern for the women of Seneca Falls, is still very much open to debate. A magazine dated February 15, 1985, published by a denomination just beginning to ordain women, contains a letter to the editor (not the first such or the last) that says:

> There has never been, and never will be, a scriptural basis for ordination of women. Further, you and all of those advocating this unscriptural act know it.

Well, in a way the gentleman is right. The point that he and his wing of the denomination do not take into consideration is that, in the sense in which he is using the word "ordination," there is no New Testament basis for ordaining *men,* either.

The priests of the Old Testament were "ordained," that is, anointed or officially installed to that office. The leaders of the church in the New Testament, such as Peter and Timothy, were not. It was not necessary then, and some Christians feel that it is not necessary today, for preachers to take courses in a seminary or to be examined on their "book learning" by a panel of experts before they can be called ministers. The whole thing was a matter of hearing God's call, directly from the lips of Jesus, such as Peter, or indirectly by the leading of the Spirit.

Women, too, felt the call to preach the gospel. As a clergyman friend of mine said, "The whole matter was settled when Jesus told the woman at the well in Samaria to go back to her village and tell everyone that she had seen the Messiah." Women, who had been last at the cross, were first at the tomb, and ran back to tell the world that the tomb was empty and that they had seen the risen Lord. True, they were not ordained, but neither was Paul. As we shall see, many women in the Bible, both Old and New Testaments, were prophets; that is, they told others about God.

In the nineteenth century women who felt called to speak about their faith in public were usually forbidden to do so in traditional circumstances, such as in churches or revivals. But, as we saw in Chapter 6, women were accepted as carriers of God's word when they became missionaries in foreign countries, either as wives of missionaries or as single women who were sent.

Antoinette Brown (Blackwell) is usually credited with being the first woman in history to be fully ordained to the Christian ministry. Arriving at Oberlin College in Ohio in 1846, she completed the "ladies' course" in one year and enrolled in the theological course, completing it in 1850. The school refused to grant her a degree or to encourage her ordination.

Understandably, she wanted to see for herself what the Bible had to say on the subject of women in leadership positions, and if possible to convince others that she had a right to take this step. She wrote an article on Paul's teaching entitled "Suffer not women to speak in the Church," published in the *Oberlin Review* in July 1849. The reference is to 1 Corinthians 14:34–35 (KJV), in which Paul says, "Let your women keep silence in the churches: for it is not permitted unto them to speak; but *they are commanded* to be under obedience, as also saith the law. And if they will learn any thing, let them ask their husbands at home: for it is a shame for women to speak in the church."

We do not know exactly what Brown wrote, but in a letter to Lucy Stone, she said:

> I have been examining the Bible position of women a good deal this winter—reading various commentaries—comparing them with other & with the Bible, & hunting up every passage in the scriptures that have [sic] any bearing on the subject either far or remote. My mind grows stronger and firmer on the subject & the light comes beaming in, full of promise. Lately I have been writing out my thoughts to see if they will all hang together but have not finished yet. It is a hard subject & takes a long time to see through it, doesn't it. But "no cross no crown."[1]

These are indeed hard passages to deal with, but a few of the points Brown probably made were the discrepancy between what Paul *said* to the church in Corinth and the many references in his writings to the value of the testimony of women. Remembering that no one was "ordained" in the modern sense of the word in the first century, let us look at a few of the passages in which Paul speaks of women as his friends and co-workers.

The most outstanding, perhaps, was Priscilla. In Romans 16:3–4 (KJV), Paul asks his readers to "Greet Priscilla and Aquila my helpers in Christ Jesus: who have for my life laid down their own necks: unto whom not only I give thanks, but also all the churches of the Gentiles. Likewise greet the church that is in their house." Not only was Priscilla to be thanked by "all the churches of the Gentiles" (and we suppose this tribute was not for her submissive silence), but also she and her husband set Apollos straight (Acts 18:24–28) when he knew "only the baptism of John," and these two Christians "expounded unto him the way of God more perfectly." Paul obviously approved of this; we do not read that Aquila was praised and Priscilla blamed for doing the same thing!

Perhaps the Corinthian women to whom Paul referred in 1 Corinthians 14 were women who, through no fault of their own, had not been trained in theology. Perhaps they chattered among themselves or asked questions out loud that disrupted the service, in which "all things were to be done decently and in order" (v. 40). Perhaps Paul was encouraging them, if they had questions, to wait until they got home, where they could ask their husbands, who were, not brighter, but better educated in that day than their wives. Many of us can imagine families today in which the wives are by far the better expositors of Scripture than the husbands.

Antoinette Brown was ordained September 15, 1853, by the First Congregational Church of Butler and Savannah, Wayne County, New York. The service was held in the larger Baptist church to accommodate the crowds. The sermon was preached by Wesleyan Methodist Luther Lee, and the charge delivered by Presbyterian Gerrit Smith. Ecumenical indeed! In the sermon, Lee said, "We are not here to make a minister. It is not to confer on this our sister, a right to preach the gospel. If she has not that right already, we have no power to communicate it to her." Thus Antoinette Brown was "one of the ministers of the New Covenant, authorized, qualified and called of God to preach the gospel of his son Jesus Christ."[2]

Lee, long active in the causes of abolition and temperance, had been a major defender of the seating of women delegates, among them Brown, in the voting section of various temperance conventions. Lee argued woman's right to preach the gospel from the text Galatians 3:28—a verse also crucial for Lee's, and many others', antislavery sentiment. If there is neither slave nor free in the sight of God, so there is neither male or female.

As Sarah Grimké had said many years earlier, when women were permitted to learn Hebrew and Greek, they would be able to judge for themselves whether Scripture had been translated correctly, and so they did. Among the Bible passages that feminist scholars found to be mistranslated was Romans 16:1-2, in which Phoebe was described as a "servant." The Greek word *diakonos* is used twenty-two times in the New Testament. When it referred to a man, the translators of the King James Version translated it "disciple" or "minister"; but when it referred to a woman, such as Phoebe, the word was translated "servant." If Phoebe was a servant, Timothy was a servant, as of course both of them were, in the sense of servants of God. If Timothy was a minister, Phoebe was a minister. "Deaconess" is a somewhat better translation, however. Obviously, for those of us who do not know the original languages, translation can still get in the way of a clear understanding of Scripture.

A woman whose story is a heart-rending example of what early women went through to prepare themselves for the ministry is Anna Howard Shaw. She stands out in her generation (1847–1915) because she was not only an ordained minister but also a medical doctor, a suffragist, and an advocate of temperance. In 1876 she went to Boston to attend theological school. Here is part of her story:

> My class at the theological school was composed of forty-two young men and my unworthy self, and before I had been a member of it an hour I realized that women theologians paid heavily for the privilege of being women. The young men of my class who were licensed preachers were given free accommodations in the dormitory, and their board, at a club formed for their assistance, cost each of them only one dollar and twenty-five cents a week. For me no such kindly provision was made. I was not allowed a place in the dormitory; but instead was given two dollars a week to pay the rent of a room outside. Neither was I admitted to the economical comforts of the club, but fed myself according to my income, a plan which worked admirably when there was an income, but left an obvious void when there was not.[3]

Because Shaw's experience was no doubt typical of many other women theological students, two anecdotes will tell us what she and her sisters went through. At one point she was preaching in a series of revival meetings. Her shoes were worn out, and she had no money to buy more. She decided that this week would determine whether or not she continued her course of study: if she was paid at least five dollars, enough to feed herself and buy a pair of shoes, she would feel that God wanted her to continue. At the end of the series, "a rousing revival," the pastor complimented her on her work and said she had earned at least fifty dollars. Unfortunately, he could not afford to pay her anything at all. Leaving the church in the depths of her despair, she was stopped by an old woman. Weeping with joy, the woman told her that because of Shaw's preaching, that night her grandson had been converted. She wished she could do something to express her gratitude, but all she had to spare was five dollars. Shaw said, "It's the biggest gift I have ever had. This little bill is big enough to carry my future on its back!"[4] She did continue her seminary education, but it was not easy. Because there was much competition for paid preaching assignments, Shaw did not receive many, and was often hungry. At one point she became so weak from malnutrition that she could not climb the stairs to her classroom without stopping to rest. Here she was discovered by the superintendent of the Woman's Foreign Missionary Society. Learning what was wrong, the woman found a sponsor for Shaw who would pay for her board—three and a half dollars a week. Anna Howard Shaw never learned the name of her benefactor; later she returned the amount to the Missionary Society. Her health improved and she was graduated. Ordination was another issue; she was eventually ordained by the Methodist Protestants because the Methodist Episcopals refused to ordain women.

The Quakers and the Salvation Army accepted women as preachers generations ago, although they do not "ordain" in quite the sense that we have been using the term.

No Time for Silence, by Janette Hassey, is a gold mine of information about which evangelical churches ordained women in the early days. Some of these churches no longer do so. For example, Dwight L. Moody worked with Emma Dryer to found the Moody Bible Institute in the 1880s. Because Moody's evangelistic tours often prevented his being in Chicago to carry on the work, he appointed Dryer to supervise the Chicago Bible work.[5] The ministry flourished, supported by philanthropists such as Nettie Fowler McCormick. Women trained by Dryer visited the sick, evangelized the poor, and organized cottage prayer meetings. Dryer parted company with Moody in 1889, but over the doctrine of divine healing, not over the doctrine of women's preaching and teaching. This is interesting, in light of the fact that Stanley Gundry was fired at Moody recently because his wife, Patricia, published a book upholding Christian feminism that was objected to by supporters of the Institute.

Briefly, and without trying to explore the theological distinctions between very similar denominations, some other churches that accepted women preachers in the early days were Methodist Protestant, ordaining Anna Howard Shaw in 1881; United Brethren, granting Lydia Sexton a license to preach in 1851 and ordaining ninety-seven women between 1889 and 1901; Free Will Baptists, licensing Clarissa Danforth to preach in 1815; and Congregationalists, with the distinction of having ordained Antoinette Brown in 1853 and ordaining at least seventy-five more women before 1920.

In 1919, M. Madeline Southard founded an Association of Women Preachers, later renamed the Association of Women Ministers. She also published a journal, *Woman's Pulpit*, in the 1920s. This shows the acceptance of women clergy as professionals in the early years of the century.[6]

As Hassey points out,

> Of four institutions which mutually supported each other as well as women preachers at the turn of the century—D. L. Moody's Bible Institute in Chicago, A. B. Simpson's Christian and Missionary Alliance, Fredrik Franson's Free Church, and the Salvation Army—only the last today maintains its historic commitment to freedom for women in public ministry.[7]

Why does it matter that they used to encourage women to make use of their talents in ministry, and do not do so now? Well, for one thing, knowing this helps to refute the charge that only very liberal churches have been open to women's leadership. The ones Hassey names were and are Bible-based, evangelical, and evangelistic. And women did for years prophesy in these denominations; that is, they did indeed expound unto their hearers "the way of God more perfectly" (Acts 18:26).

Even today, the ordination of women is not universally approved. Many of our Christian sisters are still struggling with the problem, and any step in that direction is to be regarded as a victory. In some denominations women are taking such small steps as receiving the right to vote in congregational meetings. But it's a start. The women of Seneca Falls never dreamed that it would be so long before their objection to men's "claiming Apostolic authority for [woman's] exclusion from the ministry" would be recognized as valid.

Notes

1. Elizabeth Cadzen, *Antoinette Brown Blackwell* (New York: The Feminist Press, 1983), p. 41.
2. Rosemary Reuther and Rosemary Keller, ed., *Women and Religion in America*, vol. 1 (New York: Harper & Row, Publishers Inc., 1981), p. 195.
3. Anna Howard Shaw, *The Story of a Pioneer* (Millwood, N.Y.: Kraus Reprint & Periodicals, repr. of 1915 ed.), p. 83.
4. Ibid., p. 88.
5. Janette Hassey, *No Time for Silence: Evangelical Women in Public Ministry Around the Turn of the Century* (Grand Rapids, Mich.: Zondervan Publishing House, 1986), p. 34.
6. Ibid., p. 10.
7. Ibid., p. 93.

CHAPTER TWELVE

A Battle That Was Lost

The late Equal Rights Amendment (ERA) was a lot older at the time of its demise than most people think. It was introduced into Congress in December 1923, by Quaker Alice Paul, the same woman who headed up the final drive to pass the suffrage amendment. Called the Lucretia Mott amendment, after the Quaker leader who was one of the conveners of the first Women's Rights Convention in Seneca Falls, it read:

> Men and women shall have equal rights throughout the United States and every place subject to its jurisdiction.

Debate over the amendment split the women's movement, not the first rift nor the last. Though small in numbers, the National Woman's Party (NWP), led by Alice Paul, had a good deal of influence. In the campaign for the ERA, the NWP acted with the same strength of purpose it had shown during the recent successful struggle for suffrage. Other organizations mustered their forces against the ERA, at first mainly over the issue of what would happen to "protective" legislation for working women. These labor laws dealt with the length of the working day, night shifts, working conditions, weights to be lifted, and jobs considered hazardous to women's health (such as mining) or to their morals (such as working in bowling alleys or pool rooms).

Protective laws for working women differed widely from

state to state. For example, ten states had an eight-hour maximum workday; twenty states a nine-hour workday, and seventeen a ten-hour workday day. What we must remember, in a sort of quick overview of the history of organized labor, is that the workday could be and often was even longer for men, while concern for *their* safety from moving machinery, toxic fumes, explosions, fires, and the like was almost nonexistent. So the passage of protective legislation for women and the enactment and enforcement of child labor laws had been a truly praiseworthy step toward health and dignity for some workers.

With the continued rise of the labor movement, however, the health and safety of workers of both sexes began to be considered, so that there was less emphasis on the *special* protection of women. When all the workers in an industry were working an eight-hour day, when all were shielded as much as possible from life-threatening conditions, when all were provided with toilet facilities and places (and time) to eat their lunch, it was obviously less important to "give" these advantages to women. But when the highest wages were inevitably paid to workers who were on the night shift, or who installed telephones instead of being telephone operators, or who waited tables in restaurants where alcohol was served, it began to seem to many women workers that their "protection" was protecting them from advances in salary and promotions in rank that were readily available to men.

The National Woman's Party resented being called anti-labor. They also resented the way women were categorized as weak, helpless, dependent, and easily led astray. Only pregnant women and nursing mothers, they argued, needed special protection in the work place. In 1923, shortly after World War I, the party's magazine, *Equal Rights,* insisted:

> We agree fully that the mother and unborn child demand special consideration, but so does the soldier and the man maimed in industry. Industrial conditions that are suitable for a stalwart, young, unmarried woman are certainly not equally suitable to the pregnant woman or the mother of young children. Yet "welfare"

laws apply to all women alike. Such blanket legislation is as absurd as fixing industrial conditions for men on a basis of their all being wounded soldiers would be.[1]

An Equal Rights Amendment was introduced every year between 1923 and 1972; every year it was voted down. But 1972 was a landmark year for the one-hundred-twenty-four-year-old women's movement. Introduced by Congresswoman Martha Griffiths, later Lieutenant Governor of Michigan, the reborn, renamed "Alice Paul" amendment passed in Congress March 22, 1972, by an overwhelming majority and went on to the states for ratification. It read:

> Section 1. Equality of rights under the law shall not be denied or abridged by the United States or by any State on account of sex.
> Section 2. The Congress shall have the power to enforce, by appropriate legislation, the provisions of this article.
> Section 3. This amendment shall take effect two years after the date of ratification.

For the first time, old-line women's organizations, such as the League of Women Voters, the Young Women's Christian Association, the Junior League, and even the Girl Scouts, joined forces with the newer women's liberation groups to promote a common cause. Not only was the support for the amendment in Congress and in the women's community astonishing, so was the speed with which states began to ratify. Thirty-four of the necessary thirty-eight states ratified it promptly and with little opposition.

By August 1975, only four more were needed. The deadline for ratification was March 22, 1979, seven years after ERA's successful proposal. The year 1976, with its widespread commemorations of the bicentennial of the United States, was designated to emphasize the importance of ratification, and most major women's magazines dedicated their July issues to a major emphasis on "ERA Now." Many women's organizations put some economic pressure on unratified states by voting to hold conventions only in ratified states.

Just as we have almost forgotten the long, difficult battle

for the suffrage amendment, so, I think, we have almost forgotten how close the ERA amendment came to passage almost *without* a battle. But when the deadline for ratification
arrived, three more states were needed, and several states had
tried to rescind, or back out of, their previous ratification. The
deadline was extended to June 30, 1982, and there still
seemed to be hope.

Because it was the only remaining northern industrial-
ized state, most people thought of Illinois as the unratified
state most likely to ratify. Sonia Johnson, the founder of Mor-
mons for ERA (a contradiction in terms similar to Catholics
for Abortion Rights), tells us about the last-ditch effort in
1982 to get the Illinois legislature to vote favorably. Illinois
made ratification more difficult by a previously existing rule
that required three-fifths of both houses to vote for ratification. Johnson and seven other women took the extreme step
of fasting to try to get the legislators to take the issue seri-
ously. On June 22, 1982, the vote was taken in the House, but
the amendment did not have the three-fifths majority needed
for passage.[2] When June 30 arrived, it had still not become
law, and the ERA died.

Why did it die, after so promising a beginning? First of
all, who supported the amendment and who opposed it? We
shall mention a few representative and well-known ones that
supported it.

> American Academy of Religion
> American Association of University Women
> American Federation of Labor
> American Jewish Congress
> Catholic Women's Seminary Fund, Inc.
> Evangelical Women's Caucus
> Girl Scouts of America
> Housewives for ERA
> National Organization for Women
> Young Women's Christian Association
> and a number of Protestant denominations

And who was against it? Again, among others:

> Daughters of the American Revolution
> John Birch Society
> Knights of Columbus
> Mormon Church
> Young Americans for Freedom
> Happiness of Women
> Stop ERA

Some of the opponents based their opposition on the same arguments about "protective" laws that appeared in 1923 with the Lucretia Mott amendment. The last two opposing groups were founded especially to lobby against passage of the amendment (as Housewives for ERA was founded especially to lobby for it). Their objections to the amendment all ran along the lines of the opposition to the suffrage amendment—they said passage would mean the end of family life as we know it; it would mean drafting women along with men into the armed forces; it would mean that mothers would have to support their families while fathers would not; it would mean taxes would go up to pay for childcare facilities; it would mean legal abortions, homosexual marriages, and unisex locker rooms in schools.

Many proponents of the ERA questioned the sincerity of the opponents. Did the opponents really believe that passage of ERA would mean things such as changing of family life and homosexual marriages? Or were these just scare tactics to rally support? Was the opposition to the ERA, like that of the Nineteenth Amendment, funded and encouraged by vested interests who saw that this amendment would work to their disadvantage? They might have to give women the same wages and benefits that they gave men for the same work.

There was and is one objection that carried a lot of weight with many thinking people—why was the amendment really needed, now that we had all sorts of "fair play" legislation? Many states already had "equal rights" amendments to their state constitutions (which did not, incidentally, mean that men did not have to support their children); women were being admitted to the national service academies, elected to state and national office, going to work outside the home in ever-increasing numbers, and being ordained as ministers.

The answer to that argument boils down to this: what the Supreme Court can give, the Supreme Court can take away. An example is the 1973 decision legalizing abortion, a decision which is now being challenged vigorously. An amendment to the Constitution is a lot harder to change, and only one, the Eighteenth or Prohibition Amendment, has ever been repealed. The Twenty-Eighth Amendment is needed to protect the hard-won rights that women have now.

And what about the rights women do not have? At the time that the battle for ratification was raging, women working full-time, year-round, earned, on the average, fifty-nine cents for every dollar an equally qualified man earned. That figure has now (1990) risen to the magnificent sum of sixty-nine cents, about the same as the comparative figure in 1955! A woman with a college diploma earns less, on the average, than a man with a high school diploma.

A few underpaid women were and are knowingly working for "pin-money"—taking low-paying jobs, such as substitute teaching or working in the school lunch program, in order to add a little to the family income while the kids go to school. But 73 percent of working women are single, divorced, separated, deserted, or married to men who are disabled or whose income is less than the poverty level. If they want to eat, they have no opportunity to stay at home, unless they receive some form of public assistance.

Assuring young women, as previous generations were indoctrinated to believe, that they might have to work for a few years before marriage or before the first child was born, and then Prince Charming would support them handsomely for the rest of their lives, is, and perhaps has always been, madly unrealistic. An enormous number of women find themselves in the role, not of Princess Cinderella, but of the displaced homemaker. By definition that is a spouse who has been dependent on someone else's earnings for ten years or more and now finds herself (or occasionally himself) thrust rudely into the labor market, often with very outdated marketable skills and no experience acceptable to employers. For these women, sixty-nine cents is not enough!

Let us consider some other objections raised by the opponents of ERA. The argument that the amendment will endanger the God-given right of a married woman to be supported by her husband has already been partially answered. A large percentage of women do not have husbands who are able and willing to support their families. Besides, it is not true that there are laws that ensure that husbands will pay for their families' support, even if they are able. Support laws vary widely from state to state, like liquor laws and highway load limits, but the courts seldom support the rights of the dependent spouse in an on-going marriage.

An example, far from isolated, is the Nebraska court case of McGuire versus McGuire. He was a well-to-do rancher, and they had been married for fourteen years. She worked hard in the fields, barns, and house. He had given her no money for clothes for years. The house had no running water for bathroom or kitchen sink, the furnace did not work, and her only transportation was a very old truck with no heater.

Mrs. McGuire appealed to the district court to get her husband to spend money on some of these amenities, which he could well afford to do. The decision was that he should have the house repaired, buy her a dependable car with a heater, and give her a regular monthly allowance of ten dollars. He appealed, saying that his wife was entitled only to what he decided to give her. The Nebraska Supreme Court agreed with *the husband.*

The court's majority opinion said, "The standard of living of a family is a matter of concern to the household and not for the courts to determine even though the husband's attitude toward his wife, according to his wealth and circumstances, leaves little to be said on his behalf." In order for the wife to bring action "the parties must be legally separated or living apart." This is the "protective" law of the land, or at least of some of the land, that people fear would be taken away from them if the ERA passed.[3]

As for the question of the draft: (a) There is not selective military service for anybody now. (b) If the draft were reinstated and the ERA were part of the Constitution, some women would no doubt be drafted, and they would have the same possibilities for deferment as young men—students, conscientious objectors, sole supporters of aged parents, and members of necessary civilian occupations. (c) Thousands of young women are already volunteering in the armed forces and studying in the service academies. They see these careers as opportunities for advancement and expressions of patriotism, just as young men do. It is to be hoped that women, as well as men, want to serve their country in its time of need. Remember Susan B. Anthony telling Horace Greeley that she could serve her country as he did—at the point of a quill pen?

The group Housewives for ERA, founded by Anne Bowen Follis to support the amendment, was made up of Christian homemakers (Follis is a minister's wife) who saw the need for legislation to protect the rights of all women.[4] Stop ERA was founded by Phyllis Schlafly, a woman who went to law school when the youngest of her six children was two years old. It seems ironic that a woman who combined motherhood with a successful career would be the spokesperson for an organization that promoted the status quo of traditional female roles.

The unratified states were mostly in the South, although Illinois, Nevada, Utah, and Arizona were still holdouts. When an unratified state was to vote on the amendment, women members of the opposition would go to the legislature in long formal gowns, bringing loaves of homemade bread to give to the legislators. "We don't want to be liberated!" seems to have been the cry of the anti-ERA movement. Why did they feel so threatened? Rachel Conrad Wahlberg, writing in the *Christian Century* (October 1, 1975), spoke to this point. They are afraid of multiple options, she says. Traditionally, women have been conditioned not to think independently about what to do with their lives. They are afraid of freedom, afraid of growth, afraid of responsibility. When the broom gets out of the closet, who knows whether the apprentice can control it?

If family roles are changing, and they are, they are changing without the amendment. Even if a woman belongs to a "traditional" family, a smaller segment of the American scene than ever before, that does not guarantee that she will never work outside of the home or that she will be treated equitably after divorce or widowhood. Women do live longer, on the average, than men and represent a very much larger percentage of those living in poverty. Not all of the message of the women of Seneca Falls is coming through loud and clear to the women of today, let alone to the men in power.

Notes

1. William L. O'Neill, *Everyone Was Brave* (New York: New York Times Books, 1969), p. 279.
2. Sonia Johnson, *Going Out of Our Minds: The Metaphysics of Liberation* (Freedom, Calif.: The Crossing Press, 1987).
3. Ellen Switzer, "ERA: Myth and Fact," in *Family Circle,* July 1976.
4. Anne Bower Follis, *I'm Not a Women's Libber, But . . .* (Nashville: Abingdon Press, 1981).

CHAPTER THIRTEEN

The "New" Women's Rights Movement

Americans, it seems, are very fond of reinventing the wheel. As we follow the history of education, for instance, there are periodical "discoveries" of old practices, such as teaching reading by the phonic method or requiring all college freshmen to take some basic liberal arts courses. Wow! Why didn't anybody ever think of that before? The answer, of course, is that people did think of that before, then the pendulum swung away, and now it is swinging back.

After the adoption of the Nineteenth Amendment, many women, feeeling as if their aim had been accomplished, stopped working at being feminists. Eventually, the well-known pendulum began to swing again. The women of Seneca Falls would have been astonished if they had come back between 1920 and 1960 to find women who had forgotten that they have the need for equal opportunity, human dignity, individual identity, and freedom of choice.

The generally recognized beginning of the "new" women's movement was the publication in 1963 of *The Feminine Mystique,* by Betty Friedan. It must be made clear at the outset that Friedan herself had not forgotten the earlier stages of the women's movement, which she called "The Passionate Journey." The problem is that American women reading *Mystique* often responded as if to a concept that they had never heard of before. "Do you mean to say," they said, "that I, too, can be more than 'just' a wife, a mother, a housewife?"

"Yes," said Friedan, "you can and you must, for your own good and the good of those you love."

Friedan found that the doctrine that had been instilled in the young American woman of the fifties was "that the highest value and the only commitment for women is the fulfillment of their own femininity." This goal "can find fulfillment only in sexual passivity, male domination, and nurturing maternal love."[1] We mothers are, of course, to love our children, and so are fathers, but it can happen, Friedan points out, that children are over-nurtured. Middle-class mothers are often so bored in their suburban homes with all the modern household conveniences that they spend their time organizing their children. Mama, for example, doesn't play any instrument herself; she drives her children to their music lessons and sits on the bench beside them while they practice. This can have the result of frustration for both the kids and the mother— and sometimes, one supposes, for the teacher, whose pupils never take any responsibility themselves.

There are, of course, a number of corollaries to the idea of "fulfilling our feminity." One of them is the economic importance of women as consumers. If American women are indoctrinated with the idea that their appearance and the appearance of their homes and other possessions are all-important (and, perhaps more significant, if middle-class wives and mothers have almost nothing constructive to do except to decorate themselves and their homes), of course it will be good for the furniture industry, the beauty parlor establishment, the fashion trade, the appliance and automobile manufacturers, and so on and so on. "Things are in the saddle," as Emerson said so long ago, "and ride mankind." And womankind.

Women reading Friedan were inspired by her words, and a new wave of feminism began to sweep the country. As usual, sometimes the broom got out of hand and began to deliver unmanageable amounts of water. Among the "old" values that many women discarded (let us not lay all of this at Friedan's door) was volunteering. It became a common doctrine that anybody who performed any useful task for free at a hospital, a public school, or a social agency, was being "exploited." The fact that middle-class married women were the primary volunteers because they had the time, and the fact that serving as a volunteer is a useful and rewarding element in a life that may not have much else that is useful and rewarding, was for the moment disregarded.

The next step in letting the "new freedom" get out of hand was in the downgrading of marriage. In the eyes of some groups of radical feminists, marriage was the ultimate exploitation, with all the advantages accruing on the side of the husband. The thrust of one book that came out in 1974 was that the author, a wife and mother, came to the belated, or perhaps premature, conclusion that she wasn't "finding herself" in her present role. At this point, she left her husband and ten-year-old daughter to go to another city to study art history at the graduate level. I suppose one could say that we all know husbands who have made a new life for themselves by leaving their families, but one kind of irresponsibility should not justify another kind!

Also, divorce became much easier to obtain and much more common. As we remember from history, time was when a woman could obtain a divorce only by giving up all that she had brought into the marriage, including her children. Now custody of minor children is almost invariably awarded to the mother, but along with that goes financial responsibility for their support, almost always much more difficult for the mother than for the father. (Remember the sixty-nine-cent wage?) In some cases, ready access to divorce is no doubt better for all members of the family than forced continuation of a relationship involving alcoholism, drug abuse, spouse or child abuse, or unfaithfulness. But "grounds" for divorce can be, and often are, much more trivial, with neither partner really thinking through what is involved in terms of social, financial, or moral accountability.

Unlike the women of Seneca Falls, some of the new feminists seemed not at all concerned about the will of God for

them. The Christian foremothers of the women's movement
wanted to obey the law of God. In order to find out what that
law is, they turned to Matthew 22:37-40 (KJV) and read what
Christ said: "Love the Lord thy God with all thy heart, and
with all thy soul, and with all thy might . . . and love thy
neighbor as thyself." There is nothing there about making
yourself happy at the expense of anyone who gets in your way!

We must remember that there is also a sort of under-
ground movement that wishes to return women to the extremely submissive position against which the original women
of Seneca Falls were reacting. One example, among many,
was a book that came out in 1975, *The Feminine Principle,* by
Judith Miles. One paragraph will give you an idea of the flavor
of the whole book:

> One day this familiar verse acquired a heightened meaning for
> me, "Wives, be subject to your husbands, as to the Lord" (Ephe-
> sians 5:22). It couldn't mean *that!* Not as to *the Lord!* But there
> it was. I was to treat my own human husband as though *he* were
> the Lord, resident in our own humble home. This was truly
> revelatory to me. Would I ask Jesus a basically maternal question
> such as, "How are things at the office?" Would I suggest to Jesus
> that He finish some task around the house? Would I remind the
> Lord that He was not driving prudently? But it is even more
> subtle than that. Would I ever be in judgment over my Lord, over
> His taste, His opinions, or His actions? I was stunned—stunned
> into a new kind of submission.[2]

I leave it to you to consider the implications of that paragraph, both on the lives of women and on the lives of the men
in their families.

In 1974 the first widely read book with a Christian point
of view on the "new" wave of women's liberation appeared.
All We're Meant to Be, by Letha Scanzoni and Nancy Hardesty,
went to a number of publishers before being accepted by
Word Books. The book has never been out of print since and
has had great impact on the thinking of biblical Christians,
women and men, comparable to that of the Seneca Falls Resolutions in 1848.

It is astonishing to see how often several trains of thought come together independently at the same moment in history. We cannot say that this new interest in biblical feminism came as a result of the publication of *All We're Meant to Be,* or vice versa, but at about the same time, a group called Evangelicals for Social Action met in Chicago and issued the "Chicago Declaration." This statement included the following significant passage: "We acknowledge that we have encouraged men to prideful domination and women to irresponsible passivity. So we call both men and women to mutual submission and active discipleship."

Like the earliest American biblical feminists more than a hundred years before, Evangelicals for Social Action were primarily concerned with issues other than feminism, including racism, greed, and militarism. But they saw, as did our foremothers, that women cannot make headway in causes such as abolition and temperance in the nineteenth century or race relations and economic justice in the twentieth century, unless and until they are regarded as full citizens of the country and of the kingdom of God. Thus, one of the thrusts of modern evangelicalism has to be Christian feminism. (The term "biblical feminism" means essentially the same thing, except that it is used by Jewish women who are looking at the Old Testament in a new light. This is a subject that needs to be covered in a different book.) An organization that grew out of the Evangelicals for Social Action is the Evangelical Women's Caucus. See the Appendix for a statement of their beliefs.

Since *All We're Meant to Be,* many other books on the biblical role of women have been published. A partial list appears at the end of the chapter. All address these important questions: What is the biblical perspective on questions of women's role? Does the Bible make it clear that women are to be totally dependent on men for their opinions, as well as for financial support? Was Eve created to serve Adam? If not, what *is* our duty as Christian women?

At this point we need to be reminded that women's theology or scholarship on interpretation of Scripture in light of the study of history, culture, and language is not new, either. We remember what Sarah Grimké said in 1837 about the need to take a new look at the original Hebrew and Greek instead of acting as if Genesis and First Corinthians were written by the translators of the King James Version. And, indeed, when women were "admitted to the honor" of studying Hebrew and Greek, several very interesting books came out challenging traditional male commentaries (and challenging female commentaries bearing a message like that of Judith Miles). Two of these books are *God's Word to Women,* by Katherine C. Bushnell (1919), and *The Bible Status of Woman,* by Lee Anna Starr (1926). To insert a personal note, I was absolutely astonished to realize that one of them appeared when I was a baby and the other when I was eight years old. After studying the Bible all my life, I was just finding out about a different perspective.

Once again, as did our foremothers, we are taking a new look at Bible passages that seem to forbid women's participation in the world around us. As we saw in the chapter on ordination, careful translation of the original Hebrew and Greek and new knowledge about what was going on in the world at the time of the writing help us to understand the intended meaning of the Scripture.

Let us take a brief look, as an example, at the creation story. First of all, there are two stories of the creation of man and woman, one in Genesis 1:27 and one in Genesis 2:7–25. The first one says, "in the image of God created he him; male and female created he them." The second chapter of Genesis describes the creation of Eve at a slightly later time than that of Adam: "I [God] will make him an help meet for him" (v. 18). I don't know about you, but I remember that phrase as being "helpmate," and having it interpreted as someone to stand around and hand Adam what was needed for him to do the *important* work. That is not at all what the Hebrew means. The word translated "help" is the word also used in passages such as "I will lift up up mine eyes unto the hills, from whence cometh my *help.*" The word "meet" means "suitable," as in the phrase "It is truly meet and right so to do." Eve was not a subordinate handmaiden, but rather a suitable life companion in a relationship in which both partners were truly fulfilled.

Thus we see that Christian feminism, now as well as a hundred and fifty years ago, rejoices in the scriptural message that it is God's will for women, as well as men, to be all that they are meant to be. Both women and men are created in the image of God, and it is as destructive for males to feel that they are the only human beings destined to know and serve God as it is for females to feel that they are unworthy to do either.

There certainly are women who consider degrading any mention of differences between men and women. Since the differences exist, we need to understand them and work for mutual affirmation of our strengths. Fathers, as well as mothers, can care for infants. Women, as well as men, can work with blueprints and profit and loss columns. Men, as well as women, can volunteer in social agencies. Most Christian feminists agree that we are not going to solve the problems of our exploitation by exploiting others or by saying that we are not exploited at all. Among the nay-sayers to these propositions is a group formed by Beverly LaHaye, Concerned Women for America, which insists that all feminism is ungodly, including Christian feminism, and that we need to go back to the "good old days" when "Father knows best."

Let us look at the last paragraph in the seminal book *All We're Meant to Be:*

> In Isaiah 43:4–7, God says to His people: "You are precious in my eyes and honored, and I love you. . . . Bring my sons from afar and my daughters from the end of the earth, every one who is called by my name, whom I created for my glory, whom I have formed and made." Jesus said, "Whoever does the will of God is my brother and sister and mother" (Mark 3:35). God does have daughters as well as sons; Christ does have sisters as well as brothers. Now is the time for the church to recognize this—and to act upon it. That's what the Christian woman's liberation movement is all about.[3]

Amen and amen.

Books on Biblical Feminism

Gundry, Patricia. *Woman Be Free! Free to Be God's Woman.* Grand Rapids, Mich.: Zondervan Publishing House, 1977.

Mason, Maggie. *Women Like Us.* Irving, Tex.: Word Inc., 1978.

Mollenkott, Virginia Ramey. *Women, Men,* and *the Bible.* Nashville: Abingdon Press, 1977.

Scanzoni, Letha, and Nancy Hardesty. *All We're Meant to Be: A Biblical Approach to Women's Liberation.* Irving, Tex.: Word Inc., 1974.

Storkey, Elaine. *What's Right with Feminism?* Grand Rapids, Mich.: Wm. B. Eerdmans Publishing Co., 1985.

Wahlberg, Rachel Conrad. *Jesus and the Freed Woman.* Mahwah, N.J.: Paulist Press, 1978.

Notes

1. Betty Friedan, *The Feminine Mystique* (New York: Dell Publishing Co.-Bantam Doubleday Dell Publishing Group Inc., 1984), p. 43.

2. Judith Miles, *The Feminine Principle* (Minneapolis: Bethany Fellowship, 1975), p. 44.

3. Letha Scanzoni and Nancy Hardesty, *All We're Meant to Be: A Biblical Approach to Women's Liberation* (Irving, Tex.: Word Inc., 1974), pp. 208–209.

CHAPTER FOURTEEN

The "Second Stage" and After

Where are we now in the women's movement? Has the broom gotten so far out of hand that we will never be able to get it to stop and we will all be drowned in our new-found "freedom"?

Recently, I attended a very interesting conference entitled "Feminine Rites of Passage: Rediscovering Women's Wisdom." The leaders would no doubt be astonished at the perception that I found most interesting of all about the conference, because it was not what was intended.

At any rate, the conference started out with the emphasis on women's wisdom as opposed in every way to the so-called wisdom of the Judeo-Christian tradition, which the first speakers saw as the root of all our problems. As the two days of the conference went on, there was more and more participation by the thirty or so women attending, which of course is highly to be desired in a situation such as this. By the end of the second day, members of the group were opening up and sharing their experiences in a very valuable way. Many had felt great pain in their lives. Several were single parents, concerned about their children and their own futures. Others had problems with jobs, elderly parents for whom they were responsible, rites of passage of their own which they hoped to work through by some form of rediscovering women's wisdom.

But the thing that struck me most forcefully was the repeated sense of finding fellowship, help with parenting, enabling of all sorts to get through these difficult years—in some of kind of church group. Godparents were mentioned more than once as a form of extended family for their children. One or two belonged to some kind of commune, a group sharing their faith by helping one another in times of financial or emotional need. "Church" is perhaps too formal a term for what they were a part of, but it was definitely a community of faith, and the idea that they were putting behind them any connection with the Judeo-Christian tradition could not have been further from the truth.

Much later, thinking about the two days, a lot began to come together for me. If we had made a continuum with the statement "the church is patriarchal" on one end and "the women's movement is godless or demonic" on the other, most of us at the conference came together, in sisterhood and mutual helpfulness and with a new appreciation of women's wisdom, just about in the middle.

It has been said that if we have convictions that give meaning to out lives, we will find our place in the universe. It occurred to me that the whole women's movement is traveling in the direction of finding a place for ourselves in the universe. The leaders of the conference with their scorn for the idea of any kind of God working in our lives were simply behind the times. The "Second Stage" of the women's movement has gone on beyond the perception that we are now "free" from finding any meaning in our lives to the higher perception that we do have meaning in our lives which has to begin with our seeing ourselves as women, rather than as daughters, husband-hunters, wives, mothers, and grandmothers. (Yes, even grandmothers are seeing themselves as persons with goals and aspirations of their own!)

The term "Second Stage" is, of course, borrowed from the title of Betty Friedan's 1981 book. Nearly twenty years after *The Feminine Mystique* kicked off the new phase of the women's movement, Friedan took a long look at where we have been and where we are going. She is Jewish, not Christian, and I am not including her in any list of Christian feminists, but if you look carefully at *The Second Stage,* you will see that she is a lot closer than she used to be to the whole Judeo-Christian tradition. She speaks often of the need for combining love and caring with the desire for a career and the search for one's own identity. She pleads with us women not to engage in the "me first" games that men have always been in.

> What price women's equality, if its beneficiaries, by trying to beat men at their own old power games and aping their strenuous climb onto and up the corporate ladder, fall into the traps men are beginning to escape, foregoing life satisfactions basic for men and women, foreshortening their own lives . . .?[1]

She speaks feelingly of what has falsely been seen as a polarization between equality and the family. "Family" has come to be a buzz word of the right. It does not *have* to be a married couple with the father working and the mother staying home with the children. It can be, and often is, several generations or several single mothers and their children. However it is constituted, the family is, Friedan says, "the nutrient of our humanness, of all our individuality: our personhood."[2]

Friedan refers frequently to priests, ministers, and rabbis as sources of strength for women. Active church affiliation is one of the things that has helped to keep the African American family in this country strong. She also praises volunteerism, saying that she never was comfortable with the attacks on it by the NOW group in the early days, when they called it exploitation. Voluntary organizations are needed, not only to meet essential needs in the community but also to provide opportunities for useful service. The young, the retired, women just beginning to get back into the community after being home with their young children—all these women can help provide opportunities for health care, leisure activities, the arts, help for the handicapped, and the like, things that are being cut back in the tax-supported arena these days.

In a list of great voluntary service organizations, Friedan

includes Girl Scouts, Junior League, YWCA, and religious
sisterhoods—Catholic, Protestant, and Jewish. This, rightly
or wrongly, is not the image the world has had of Betty Friedan, and I, for one, take my hat off to her. Caring, nurturing,
loving—these are important areas in the lives of all men and
women, whether married, single, employed, retired, in or out
of the organized church. "Life lived only for oneself does not
truly satisfy men or women."[3]

A few years ago there was an interesting exchange of
letters in the letters to the editor column in my newspaper.
One woman writer was vociferous in her claim that all married
women whose husbands were employed should stay out of the
work force. It was all those married women working outside
the home, she said, that caused inflation and contributed to
unemployment among men. If they set their sights a little
lower, she said, and stayed home where they belonged, there
would be less juvenile delinquency and we would all be better
off. A few days later, a reply appeared, in which another
woman was equally vehement in her position that all married
women who let their husbands support them were parasites.
Where does the truth lie?

Well, for one thing, the idea that most women have any
choice in the matter is snobbish. Most married women who
are employed really need the money. The cost of a home
today, let alone the cost of educating children, is far above the
reach of most one-income families. The idea that the married
woman who works is working for a side-by-side refrigerator
freezer with ice and running water in the door is, in most
cases, nonsense. And, of course, there are millions of one-
parent homes headed by women, but, to do her justice, this
is not the kind of home the first letter writer was thinking
about.

Second, if all the employed married women stayed home
tomorrow, the world as we know it would grind to a screech-
ing halt. If hospitals, for instance, sent all the married nurses
home and hired men from the unemployment lines, as the
first letter writer seemed to imply, our health care system

would be in chaos. On the other hand, mothers who can and do stay home to take care of their families certainly are not parasites. No one who has done it could possibly deny the truth of the slogan "Every mother is a working mother"!

The percentage of wives and mothers in the work force, often the mothers of very young children, is going up all the time. The perception by a girl that some day a knight on a white horse is going to ride up and rescue her from the drudgery of the work-a-day world is becoming more and more unrealistic, and many young people realize it. There are many reasons for this: Not all women get married and not all stay married. Women live longer than men, on the average, and the divorce rate is unfortunately high, so there have to be more and more households headed by women. And even for those fortunate enough to be wives (rather than widows or divorcees) all their lives, a second income is necessary for many, many families. If there ever was a time when the average American family consisted of a father who is employed and a mother who is not, those times are gone.

Assuming that a woman can choose what she would like to do to supplement the family income and/or to make a contribution to the world, what kind of work would she like to do? Increasingly, in the second stage, women would like to turn to what Elise Boulding, in *The Underside of History,* calls altruism, and Jessie Bernard, in *The Female World,* calls agape. Loving, caring, sharing, nurturing—whatever you want to call it—is represented by the kinds of participation in the lives of others which Boulding speaks of as arising "from some inner surplus of resources."[4]

Freud told us several generations ago that the twin pillars of a mentally healthy life were love and work. As we know, Freud was probably not thinking of women, but these pillars hold up our lives as well. The trick is to determine what is ideally meant by "love" and what by "work." Love for one's husband and children is and should be a motivating force in the lives of married women, but after early childhood, what kind of love does a child need? Indeed, what parts of his work should be done for him? (I am consciously using the male child as an example here, because I think we mothers are more likely to over-mother our boys. Over-mothering girls, however, is also devastating to the daughter's future. Unfortunately, too many youngsters have few roots, but it is also true that many have no wings.)

Gail Sheehy describes this kind of human goal very effectively in her 1981 best seller, *Pathfinders.* I did not expect her to use as role models so many men and women who are dedicating their lives to some kind of greater good. Of course, Sheehy tells about the lives of people who "found themselves" in ways other than full-time Christian service, but I was struck throughout the book by the message that those who have really got it all together in today's world, sometimes late in life, were people who wanted to serve others in some way. And, when they do, they say, with the Reverend Delia Barnes, that "I feel at last a firm sense of my identity." She is described by Sheehy as "secure, not solely in her bond to parents or mate, to children, peers, or employers, but now also in her tie to the culture."[5] That is a nice kind of security to have, and one that I am sure would be applauded by the original women of Seneca Falls. What they wanted, after all, was the position "to which the laws of nature and of nature's God entitle them"!

With God's help, we will all be able to attain that position. We have firm hands on the brooms that are helping us with the drudgery, and our firebrands will be destroying the obstacles that still stand in our way. We all, both men and women, will be able to be all that God wants us to be.

Notes

1. Betty Friedan, *The Second Stage* (Englewood Cliffs, N.J.: Summit Books-Simon & Schuster Inc., 1981), p. 54.
2. Ibid., p. 178.
3. Ibid., p. 265.
4. Elise Boulding, *The Underside of History* (Boulder, Colo.: Westview Press, 1976).
5. Gail Sheehy, *Pathfinders* (New York: Bantam Books, Inc., 1982), p. 12.

Study Questions

Have Bibles handy as you discuss these matters of concern relating to each chapter. I am imagining the participants in the discussions to be female. If you are a male student of women's history, try to disregard the "sexist" phrases (after all, women have had to do that for centuries!), merely replacing key words with those that apply to you. For example, "Suppose *my wife* wants to spend her money on something I consider unnecessary or to give it away to a cause of which I do not approve?"

Chapter 1–Of Brooms and Firebrands

1. Take a moment to jot down what the phrase "women's movement" means to you. Some people, both men and women, feel threatened by the movement, perceiving it as dangerous to their faith and to their ideal of the family. Some people, both men and women, feel that it has been a blessing, that great strides are being made toward the recognition of women's contributions. There is much to be said for both points of view, and you will find, when you share what you wrote down, that you have lots of company wherever you stand. Perhaps your perception will change as you study *Hallowed Fire.* If so, it will be interesting to save what you wrote today so that you can see how it has changed.

2. You may not have thought before about the lives of

married women whose destinies were absolutely under their husbands' command, such as those women who signed the petitions presented in 1854. Imagine that your husband or father has complete control over your money and property and over the kind of lives you and your children will lead. (Or if you are not married, the lives your brothers and sisters and yourself will lead.) Of course, some husbands and fathers were and are very kind and generous, but not all! Think of a decision that you made recently. How would you feel if the men in your life had absolute veto power? Read Ephesians 5:21 to the end of the chapter. This passage has been interpreted to mean that wives and children have to submit to husbands and fathers, *no matter what.* But verse 21 (KJV) says, submit "yourselves one to another." Granted, it is not possible for everyone in the family to get his or her own way all the time, but does this passage say that it is God's will for Papa to be lord and master?

3. The Christian women you are going to read about came from a variety of denominations. Is it possible, in your view, for Christians to work together on common causes without agreeing on every religious issue? There were, and are, those who think Quakers and Episcopalians, for instance, have so many theological differences that they have nothing in common. Or perhaps they think that Quakers are not saved, or that Episcopalians are not. Have you ever been a member of a highly ecumenical organization, such as Habitat for Humanity or Church Women United? Is it up to us to decide whether others are Christians or not?

Chapter 2–The Road to Seneca Falls

1. One of the fascinating details of Lydia Maria Child's life is her (and her husband's) use of peaceful protest and economic boycott as means to combat slavery. Have you ever joined a protest march, circulated petitions, written letters to your representatives, or refused to buy products of which you did not approve? Share with the group what you did, keeping in mind that not everybody will agree on the cause you espoused or the stand you took. That's all right!

2. We will return to the concept of "a perverted application of Scripture," but let us begin by thinking about that word "perverted." Discuss how you would answer this charge: If we begin thinking about Bible verses in a different way than they have been applied before, *we* are the ones who are perverting Scripture. Can you think of rules that were universal in Bible times that we do not pay any attention to now because conditions have changed? One example, to get us started, might be the custom of washing the feet of guests who come to your house for dinner. I can't help picturing the scene if I offered a basin and a towel to someone who came to my door all dressed up! (Of course, the perception of helpfulness and hospitality still holds.) Think of other Bible passages that fall into this "changing times" category. Does it bother you to think that we do not take *every word* at face value? Why or why not?

3. Does "work for women to do *beyond* the bounds of hearth and nursery" mean that women are *not* supposed to cook or change diapers? Discuss some of the changes in modern households that might mean that we can, and often do, get the housework done and also have "work to do" (paid or volunteer) beyond the bounds of our own family's needs. And what about the idea of husbands doing some of the cooking and diaper changing? After the kids are toddlers, do you think it might be good for *them* to have a mother who has a life of her own and is too busy to wait on the kids hand and foot?

Chapter 3–Seneca Falls

1. The women of Seneca Falls proposed to discuss the "social, civil, and religious conditions and rights of women" at their 1848 convention. Discuss the proposition that we sometimes get ourselves all in a twist about one of those three realms, while forgetting about the others. What happens when any group—women, organized labor, politicians, whatever—concerns itself entirely with social and civil rights without taking religion into consideration? It is interesting to note that the Declaration of Sentiments put a lot of emphasis on religious conditions and rights. Do you think the women at Seneca Falls overlooked social and civil conditions of their day? Think about the phrase "conditions and rights." Do we sometimes get too concerned about our rights without enough concern about conditions—for example, our responsibilities as wife and mother, or church member, or citizen?

2. The summing up refers to our capabilities and our responsibility for their exercise. What happens when a very gifted person is *unable* to use his or her God-given talents? What happens when he or she seems to be *unwilling* to use the talents? Does the parable of the talents (Matthew 25) have some relevance here? It might be interesting to share some personal experiences about the problems of deciding what has priority in a very busy life. If there are older people in the group, discuss how and when (and if) one's life becomes somewhat less complicated!

3. Galatians 3:28 was a rallying cry for the cause of abolition. Read it together and discuss the ways in which the implications of the verse encourage other causes besides antislavery. Do you think Paul meant that there were neither slaves nor free persons in his day? If not, what does he mean? How are these words consistent with other "proof texts" that seem to show that Paul wanted slaves and women to be subservient? Do you think the verses about how women are to conduct themselves in public might be part of the culture of the day, such as the verses about not eating meat offered to idols?

Chapter 4–"Jesus Loves Me, This I Know"

1. The whole idea of the "benevolent empire" deserves some careful thought. Obviously, many of the women who were active in philanthropic endeavors were well endowed with money and with time to act out all these charitable impulses. Sarah Doremus in Chapter 6, for example, had servants to take care of her nine children. But some of them were not so endowed. Discuss the story of Katy Ferguson, for example. She was poor and she was an African American, but she was opening her arms to underprivileged children of all races. Does this invert the picture of the "lady bountiful," busily forcing changes on the lifestyles of the poor (so they would be more like her) and expecting them to be grateful for it? Perhaps today's picture of the society matron who hopes to get her name in the news by her good works is too uncharitable. What do you think?

2. Read Mark 9:36–37 and 10:13–16. Do you suppose the origins of the Sunday school movement arose in verses such as these? Can you think of other passages dealing with the treatment of small children? How do you feel about waiting until youngsters have reached an age of discretion before giving them any religious instruction? Obviously, four-year-olds cannot be fed the same spiritual food as fourteen-year-olds, but those who teach little ones are often astonished at their untutored insights. One little boy, asked what he thought death would be like, said, "Sometimes when we are coming home from grandma's, I fall asleep in the car, and when I wake up I am all tucked up in bed and I didn't even know it. I guess dying is going to be like that; I'll wake up safe and sound in heaven!" Do you know of other instances of children's understandings?

3. How do you feel about the Sunday school materials you were exposed to as a child, or, if you are a teacher of small children or have small children who bring their papers home, how do you feel about the materials used today? How do you feel about "International Lessons," materials that are supplied in four-year cycles? What seems to you to be an appropriate curriculum for an adult Sunday school class?

Chapter 5–Louisa and Harriet, for Example

1. In *In Search of Our Mothers' Gardens*, Alice Walker says, "I had that wonderful feeling writers get sometimes, not very

often, of being with a great many people, ancient spirits, all
very happy to see me consulting and acknowledging them,
and eager to let me know, through the joy of their presence,
that, indeed, I am not alone."[1]

Walker is speaking of discovering for the first time that
there have been many African American women poets. Do
you feel something of this "wonderful feeling" when you
think of the "ancient spirits" of the Christian women who
have been so instrumental in working to improve the lives of
women in the United States? Please share with the group
something about Christian women you have known or read
about who let you know, by the joy of their presence, that you,
as a biblical feminist, are not alone.

2. Today, some people say that the modern wife and
mother of young children works just as hard, for just as many
hours, as Harriet (for instance) did because so many tasks
have been added, such as chauffeuring the kids to all kinds of
sporting events. Do you agree? Take laundry, for instance. It
is certainly easier with automatic water heaters, automatic
washers and dryers, and permanent-press fabrics. But we do
seem to have a lot more of it! Everybody in the family changes
clothes from the skin out every day, sometimes more than
once a day. Does Mother, or whoever does the laundry, have
more to do than she did a hundred years ago? If so, would it
be possible to arrange our lives more wisely?

3. I'm sure you have read the description of the "virtuous
woman" in Proverbs 31 many times, or had it read to you in
Mother's Day sermons. Reread it now and see if there are any
features of her life that surprise you. For example, was it ever
pointed out to you that she was a dealer in real estate (v. 16)
or a designer of women's clothing (v. 24)? ("Girdles" is sometimes translated "sashes" or "belted garments." It certainly
did not mean corsets!) Also, "she openeth her mouth with
wisdom" (v. 26); her husband is not the only wise and
thoughtful person in the family. Does this give you a different
idea of the "virtuous wife" than you had before? Obviously,
she is almost too good to be true, but we can see that she is

praised for other things as well as for spinning and weaving and preparing food for her household. Just like most of today's married women, she has a career!

Chapter 6–To India's Coral Strand

1. Many missionaries, and many supporters of missionaries, have been inspired by Romans 10:13–17. We also have the words of Christ to the disciples, Mark 16:15. Matthew 10:5 and the verses following are a very detailed blueprint of what Christ expected of his disciples. Thinking of *foreign* missions for the moment, how well do you think the church today is fulfilling these commands? Foreign missions have been severely criticized, perhaps justly, for sending missionaries who expect to change the native people's dress, diet, table manners, and so forth, rather than accepting the cultural differences. On the other hand, Christians have established such things as hospitals, orphanages, and markets for handcrafts. On the whole, are we doing more harm than good? If so, what can those of us who are the church do about it?

2. Why do you think it was easier for the male-dominated churches of the mid-nineteenth century to accept women foreign missionaries than to accept women in the pulpits of their own churches? Agree or disagree with the proposition that women had to succeed in the foreign field before main-line denominations could accept them as preachers at home.

3. The nineteenth century was a time of active colonialism. White people tended to see the yellow, black, and red races as basically inferior and in need of improved values and lifestyles as well as of the message that Jesus loves them. For instance, in the hymn from which the title of the chapter is taken ("From Greenland's Icy Mountains"), Reginald Heber writes, "Can we to men benighted the lamp of life deny?" and Kipling, in "Recessional," wrote of "the lesser breeds without the law." How has the role of missionaries changed? What type of work is done by missionaries who are supported by your church?

Chapter 7–Down With Demon Rum!

1. You will not all agree, but how do you feel about the "responsible" use of alcohol? Is a glass of beer on a hot day or a glass of wine with dinner necessarily bad for everyone? Could it be compared with a piece of chocolate candy at the end of a meal, as opposed to eating the whole pound box? Look up some of the uses of the word "wine" in a concordance. Jesus turned water into wine (and good wine it was, too!) and spoke of new wine and old wine in wineskins. It is also historic fact that water was not always potable in many parts of the world. On the other hand, we have Paul's admonition in Romans 14:13 against putting a stumbling block in our brother's or sister's path; in other words, we need to be a good example for those who might not be able to handle drinking, or whatever the occasion of sin we are talking about might be. We are not, I think, talking about underage drinking or driving while drunk, but just about whether Christians must be total abstainers, and why.

2. Why do you think the cause of temperance was so popular with Christian women in the nineteenth century? The WCTU was the largest women's organization in terms of numbers of members in the United States. Why do you think there is a recent trend for people today to join causes similar to the WCTU, for example, Mothers Against Drunk Driving? What seems to you the best way for the family and the church, working together, to combat addiction, whether it be to alcohol, drugs, or tobacco?

3. It is often said that our actions speak louder than our words. In what ways do adults sometimes set a bad example for the young? Consider today's advertising. Can you think of ways in which people are encouraged to look for some way to escape from pain or boredom or unpopularity in pills or cocktails? How about "losing oneself" in activities? Is anyone being encouraged to "find" himself or herself?

Chapter 8–It's a Man's World Until Women Vote

1. Thinking about Susan B. Anthony's letter to the president of the California WCTU, do you think she was right about considering the issue of suffrage apart from the matter of what the women were going to vote for? Most people of that day thought of votes for women as potentially changing something; passage of the amendment was tied in with prohibition, or world peace, or whatever. But it was actually about the right to vote "yea or nay on each and all" of these issues. How is this like choosing candidates on the basis of their stand on abortion, for example? How is it like deciding how to vote on the Equal Rights Amendment on the basis of the voter's perception of what its supporters were like or what they stood for? How do you decide how to vote on a hotly contested issue?

2. Like it or not, we are going to be influenced by the image of the supporters of an issue—Carry Nation and prohibition, for instance, or Victoria Woodhull and women's rights. Can you think of any contemporary figures whose opinions or appearance or manner of speaking turn you off when you think of voting for them or voting for what they stand for? (Or perhaps, you vote for someone because of her image.) To what extent is this justified?

3. Do you think the pulpit or a denominational publication is the place for political advice? Why or why not? Do Christians need to think about the social and economic consequences of American political actions? Is this a matter for the church to direct? Once again, you will not all agree; it is often interesting to hear arguments for both sides.

Chapter 9–Emancipation from the Crinoline

1. The Bible was brought into play here as verses were quoted that seem to regulate the way women dress or the way they wear their hair. Read 1 Corinthians 11:1–15. Leaving aside for the moment what Paul meant by "head" (a very important question, but not relevant to the matter of dress!), how do you feel about the matters of long hair and head coverings? Not long ago (and still in some churches) no woman went to church without a hat, although most women did not wear one all the time. Do you think this was a command or just a response to the customs of the day? In Corinth, in the first century, only prostitutes went out on the street bare-headed. I guess if someone thought I was a prostitute because of my hatless state, I'd hurry up and buy a hat!

2. Following this line of thought, do you think Christian women are commanded to have long hair? As some of you will remember, the sixties saw many pitched battles between fathers and sons about the *boys* wanting to wear their hair long. Is this, in your opinion, a matter to make an issue of (assuming that they washed and combed it)? Why or why not? Read 1 Timothy 2:9. If we follow this advice to its ultimate conclusion, women with long hair should not braid it! Do you think this is what Paul meant, or is the emphasis on "gold, pearls, and costly array?" What does this mean about costly array in today's terms, and does it apply to men as well?

3. Think about the horror with which "trousers" for women (really long divided garments gathered around the ankles so that the wearer could move freely) were greeted. How about cultures in which the men wear "skirts"—that is, long robes? How about the vestments of many of the male clergy? As long as one is decently clothed (and of course not all agree on what *that* means) do you think skirts or trousers are a theological matter? Why or why not?

Chapter 10–The Dangerous Experiment

1. Education for women, like votes for women, was often preached against on the ground that it would mean the end of the Christian family. Women who had been to college, it was said, would never be willing to settle down and raise a family. Suggest some arguments for and against this perception. Do you know any women who went to college, married, stayed home with their children, and then went out to work in their chosen careers? What happened? What would you say would be the ideal point in a marriage for the wife and mother (assuming she could afford to stay home at all) to go to work? What are the advantages and disadvantages for part-time jobs for married women? A nontraditional approach might be for *both* parents to work part-time, or even to share a job so that one was always home when the kids were small. Do you think this would work?

2. An argument for women's higher education that was popular a generation ago was that she would make a better wife and mother if she had more intellectual interests, as opposed to a woman who cared about nothing but house-work. She could, for example, help her children with their homework. How do you feel about this? Is this good enough motivation? Should a woman be prepared to take a job "in case" she needs to make a living some day? Is this good enough motivation? (We are assuming, of course, that she wants to go to college.) What if she has intellectual interests and her husband has none? What if he has intellectual interests and she has none?

3. Some men feel threatened by the idea that their wives have interests and money that the men do not provide. Look at the account in Acts 18 of the lives of Priscilla and Aquila. Do you think the author of Acts approves of their activities? What did the couple do for a living? Who else in the Christian church had the same trade? Were their activities in the church shared, too? Was it obvious that one or the other was the leader? There is a group of men called the "Aquila Society" that affirms the concept of shared lives. Assuming that they are not putting this obligation on all Christian families, do you think the "Aquilas" are right?

Chapter 11–Your Daughters Shall Prophesy

1. Let's look up some of the Bible passages that have been used for and against the idea of ordaining women. The title of the chapter comes from Acts 2:14–18, a sermon preached by Peter on the day of Pentecost. Peter, it is clear, is quoting Scripture himself: Joel 2:28–29. If as far back as Joel the message was proclaimed that "your sons *and your daughters* shall prophesy," and if Peter used this passage in one of his most important sermons, the idea of women in the ministry should not be appalling to any of us! Of course, the question arises, what does it mean to prophesy? The Bible is speaking about revealing the will or message of God—preaching, particularly preaching the gospel of Christ. Paul, in 1 Corinthians 14:3, says, "He who prophesies speaks to men [that is, Christians] for their upbuilding and encouragement and consolation." Surely, women too can upbuild, encourage, and console! Read the rest of Peter's sermon and discuss what seems to you to be involved in the visitation of the Holy Spirit on this memorable day and what it means to us today. Whatever it is, it is very clear that it is not a gift given to men only!

2. There were lots of prophets in the Old Testament; the word "prophet" is used over three hundred times, but they were all men, weren't they? No, they weren't. Miriam, the sister of Moses, is described in Exodus 15:20 as a prophetess. Deborah, Judges 4:4–10, was also a prophetess, and "the people of Israel came to her for judgment." Perhaps the most remarkable woman of all is probably the least known. In 2 Kings 22, Huldah was consulted about a "book of the law," which she read and interpreted for the high priest and a scribe. One reason this is so strange is that although both Jeremiah and Zephaniah were alive and available, none of Huldah's contemporaries seemed to think that it was remarkable that these emissaries of King Josiah came to her and accepted her "Thus says the LORD, the God of Israel" without question. How did she know what the fragment of manuscript meant? The same way the other prophets knew what to say— God told her. Do you think we can disregard this story today? Why do you think it has been disregarded by many Bible scholars?

3. Read Philippians 4:2–3. Have you ever heard a sermon about Euodia and Syntyche? If you have, it's likely that you heard that they couldn't get along together. Paul urged them to "be of the same mind," to "agree," to "quarrel no more," depending on the translation. True, they had not agreed. Paul and Barnabas, too, disagreed (see Acts 15:39), but is that the only thing we know about them? Then why is it the only thing we remember about Euodia and Syntyche? We are also told that they "labored side by side . . . in the gospel" and their names, along with Paul's other fellow laborers, are "in the book of life." Sometimes we are criticized for objecting to commentaries that overlook the good points to stress the unfortunate ones. I have had people say to me, "Don't be so hard on him; he didn't do it on purpose!" I guess that's worse. Prejudice against women or people of another race or people who speak another language, or whatever, is sometimes so ingrained that we do not even know we are prejudiced. Let's hear it for Euodia and Syntyche!

Chapter 12–A Battle That Was Lost

1. In the early years of the ERA amendment, an important issue was the potential loss of women's protective legislation (dealing with such things as special job conditions) as opposed to women's rights to compete for higher-paying, "nontraditional" jobs. Do you feel that women need special protection, or are the safety rules laid down by OSHA and other agencies sufficient to protect both men and women? If you were counseling a young, healthy woman who wanted, for example, to get off the welfare rolls, would you advise her to prepare herself for a nontraditional job? Why or why not?

2. We considered earlier the issue of supporting or opposing an issue solely on the basis of what *we* hope will come of it. For example, some suffagists worked for getting the vote because they hoped a prohibition amendment would then be passed. Do you think there were any elements of this kind of thinking by the supporters or opponents of the ERA? Give some examples, and discuss the validity of their point of view.

3. Read together the partial list of groups supporting or opposing the ERA. You will not all agree, but how do you feel about being on the side, for example, of the John Birch Society? On the side of the National Organization for Women (NOW)? Why do you think any particular organization that existed before the amendment was proposed chose to support it or oppose it? What do you consider the main reason the amendment was defeated?

Chapter 13–The "New" Women's Rights Movement

1. Richard Quebedeaux, in *The Worldly Evangelicals,* calls biblical feminism a product of the secular women's movement of the late '60s and '70s. He says it is "a profound instance of the world's setting the agenda for the church, rather than vice versa."² Do you think this is true? If not, can you think of other examples of "new" programs that are "new" only because most people do not remember their history? Why is it important to recognize the real roots of a movement before we brand it as modern nonsense with no biblical foundation?

2. Realizing that you are not all going to see this in exactly the same way, how do you feel about the two creation stories? Read the relevant sections of Genesis 1 and 2; can you see any justification for *two* stories? For example, do you see Genesis as a textbook for geology and anthropology or as a deeply significant investigation of *why* humankind appeared on the earth and what is expected of men and women now? This is slightly flippant, but does it seem to you likely that God would have created male and female examples of all the other animals and only a male of humankind? "It is not good for man to be alone," is a beautiful thought; but if he had been alone, there would never have been another of his kind, would there? Does the Hebrew meaning of "help meet" change your mind about Eve's purpose for being?

3. Take a look at the quotation from Judith Miles and at Ephesians 5: 22, the passage on which it is based. Do you think the verse means what Miles thinks it means? Why or why not? Give serious consideration to whether or not we are to

look up to any human being in the same way that we look up
to the Lord. Would that constitute idolatry? Do we worship
our pastor? our president? our country? If not, are we supposed to worship our husbands? If we did, how would this
affect the husband? We are told "not to think of himself more
highly than he ought to think" (Romans 12:3); one wonders
how a man would think of himself (at home) if faced every day
with such unquestioning acceptance of his every word and
deed. If you are familiar with *The Total Woman,* by Marabel
Morgan, compare her handling of her marriage with Miles'.

Chapter 14–The "Second Stage" and After

1. Today, many people feel that the broom has indeed
carried in more water than we can handle and that this
"woman question" has gone *too far!* I suppose most of us
would agree to some extent with that proposition. Our biggest problem is deciding which bucketsful are too much. Possible examples of "too much" might be ease of obtaining a
divorce, acceptance of premarital sex, acceptance of abortion,
careers for mothers of very young children, ease of obtaining
addictive substances, and on and on. Realizing that you are
not all going to agree about what is "too much" (for example,
was it better when divorce was so unthinkable that some married couples lived together for years without speaking to one
another?), bring up some of the things that seem to you to be
the result of going overboard on this "rights" thing. Is there
any way of resolving the dilemma without going back to the
"good old days," when children spoke only when spoken to
and wives were always broke, barefoot, and pregnant?

2. Do you agree that we must find our own place in the
universe? Do you agree that we can? Give some examples
from your own life or those you have read about or met who
have been able to "stand the most incredible hardships."
What, for example, gave people the strength to survive con-
centration camps or unjust prison sentences? Is there more
to it than just belief in God?

3. Friedan speaks of the family as "the nutrient of our humanness, of all our individuality: our personhood." Is there any sense in which the family may be a detriment to our personhood? Have you ever known anyone who was *just* a mother? anyone who gave her children roots but no wings? What happens, or what do you think will happen, when her children are all grown? Do you know anyone who has been able to share his or her loving, caring, and nurturing skills with others besides just his or her own family? Describe the values this "tie to the culture" has for (a) the nurturer and (b) the nurtured.

Notes

1. Alice Walker, *In Search of Our Mothers' Gardens, Womanist Prose* (Orlando: Harcourt Brace Jovanovich Inc., 1984), p. 13.
2. Richard Quebedeaux, *The Worldly Evangelicals* (San Francisco: Harper & Row Publishers, Inc., 1978), p. 126.

APPENDIX

Seneca Falls Convention
Declaration of Sentiments

When, in the course of human events, it becomes necessary for one portion of the family of man to assume among the people of the earth a position different from that which they have hitherto occupied, but one to which the laws of nature and of nature's God entitle them, a decent respect for the opinions of mankind requires that they should declare the causes that impel them to such a course.

We hold these truths to be self-evident: that all men and women are created equal; that they are endowed by their Creator with certain inalienable rights; that among these are life, liberty, and the pursuit of happiness; that to secure these rights governments are instituted, deriving their just powers from the consent of the governed. Whenever any form of government becomes destructive of these ends, it is the right of those who suffer from it to refuse allegiance to it, and to insist upon the institution of a new government, laying the foundation on such principles, and organizing its powers in such form, as to them shall seem most likely to effect their safety and happiness. Prudence indeed, will dictate that governments long established should not be changed for light and transient causes, and accordingly all experience hath shown that mankind are more disposed to suffer, while evils are sufferable, than to right themselves by abolishing the forms to which they were accustomed. But when a long train of abuses and usurpations, pursuing invariably the same object evinces a design to reduce them under absolute despotism, it is their duty to throw off such government, and to provide new guards for their future security. Such has been the patient sufferance of the women under this government, and such is now the necessity which constrains them to demand the equal station to which they are entitled.

The history of mankind is a history of repeated injuries and usurpations on the part of man toward woman, having in direct object the establishment of an absolute tyranny over her. To prove this, let facts be submitted to a candid world.

He has never permitted her to exercise her inalienable right to the elective franchise.

He has compelled her to submit to laws, in the formation of which she had no voice.

He has withheld from her rights which are given to the most ignorant and degraded men—both natives and foreigners.

Having deprived her of this first right of a citizen, the elective franchise, thereby leaving her without representation in the halls of legislation, he has oppressed her on all sides.

He has made her, if married, in the eye of the law, civilly dead.

He has taken from her all right in property, even to the wages she earns.

He has made her, morally, an irresponsible being, as she can commit many crimes with impunity, provided they be done in the presence of her husband. In the covenant of marriage, she is compelled to promise obedience to her husband, he becoming, to all intents and purposes, her master—the law giving him power to deprive her of her liberty, and to administer chastisement.

He has so framed the laws of divorce, as to what shall be the proper causes, and in case of separation, to whom the guardianship of the children shall be given, as to be wholly regardless of the happiness of women—the law, in all cases, going upon a false supposition of the supremacy of man, and giving all power into his hands.

After depriving her of all rights as a married woman, if single and the owner of property, he has taxed her to support a government which recognizes her only when her property can be made profitable to it.

He has monopolized nearly all the profitable employments, and from those she is permitted to follow, she receives but a scanty remuneration. He closes against her all the avenues to wealth and distinction which he considers most honorable to himself. As a teacher of theology, medicine, or law, she is not known.

He has denied her the facilities for obtaining a thorough education, all colleges being closed against her.

He allows her in Church, as well as State, but a subordinate position, claiming Apostolic authority for her exclusion from the ministry, and, with some exceptions, from any public participation in the affairs of the Church.

He has created a false public sentiment by giving to the world a different code of morals for men and women, by which moral delinquencies which exclude women from society, are not only tolerated, but deemed of little account in man.

He has usurped the prerogative of Jehovah himself, claiming it as his right to assign for her a sphere of action, when that belongs to her conscience and to her God.

He has endeavored, in every way that he could, to destroy her confidence in her own powers, to lessen her self-respect, and to make her willing to lead a dependent and abject life.

Now, in view of this entire disfranchisement of one-half the people of this country, their social and religious degradation—in view of the unjust laws above mentioned, and because women do feel themselves aggrieved, oppressed, and fraudulently deprived of their most sacred rights, we insist that they have immediate admission to all the rights and privileges which belong to them as citizens of the United States.

In entering upon the great work before us, we anticipate no small amount of misconception, misrepresentation, and ridicule; but we shall use every instrumentality within our power to effect our object. We shall employ agents, circulate tracts, petition the State and National legislatures, and endeavor to enlist the pulpit and the press in our behalf. We hope this Convention will be followed by a series of Conventions embracing every part of the country.

Seneca Falls Resolutions

WHEREAS, The great precept of nature is conceded to be, that "man shall pursue his own true and substantial happiness," Blackstone in his Commentaries remarks, that this law of Nature being coeval with mankind, and dictated by God himself, is of course superior in obligation to any other. It is binding over all the globe, in all countries and at all times; no human laws are of any validity if contrary to this, and such of them as are valid, derive all their force, and all their validity, and all their authority, mediately and immediately, from this original; therefore:

Resolved, That such laws as conflict, in any way, with the true and substantial happiness of woman, are contrary to the great precept of nature and of no validity, for this is "superior in obligation to any other."

Resolved, That all laws which prevent woman from occupying such a station in society as her conscience shall dictate, or which place her in a position inferior to that of man, are contrary to the great precept of nature, and therefore of no force or authority.

Resolved, That woman is man's equal—was intended to be so by the Creator, and the highest good of the race demands that she should be recognized as such.

Resolved, That the women of this country ought to be enlightened in regard to the laws under which they live, that they may no longer publish their degradation by declaring themselves satisfied with their present position, nor their ignorance, by asserting that they have all the rights they want.

Resolved, That inasmuch as man, while claiming for himself intellectual superiority, does accord to woman moral superiority, it is pre-eminently his duty to encourage her to speak and teach, as she has an opportunity, in all religious assemblies.

Resolved, That the same amount of virtue, delicacy, and refinement of behavior that is required of woman in the social state, should also be required of man, and the same transgressions should be visited with equal severity on both man and woman.

Resolved, That the objection of indelicacy and impropriety, which is so often brought against woman when she addresses a public audience, comes with a very ill-grace from those who encourage, by their attendance, her appearance on the stage, in the concert, or in feats of the circus.

Resolved, That woman has too long rested satisfied in the circumscribed limits which corrupt customs and a perverted application of the Scriptures have marked out for her, and that it is time she should move in the enlarged sphere which her great Creator has assigned her.

Resolved, That it is the duty of the women of this country to secure to themselves their sacred right to the elective franchise.

Resolved, That the equality of human rights results necessarily from the fact of the identity of the race in capabilities and responsibilities.

Resolved therefore, That, being invested by the Creator with the same capabilities, and the same consciousness of responsibility for their exercise, it is demonstrably the right and duty of woman, equally with man, to promote every righteous cause by every righteous means; and especially in regard to the great subjects of morals and religion, it is self-evidently her right to participate with her brother in teaching them, both in private and in public, by writing and by speaking, by any instrumentalities proper to be used, and in any assemblies proper to be held; and this being a self-evident truth growing out of the divinely implanted principles of human nature, any custom or authority adverse to it, whether modern or wearing the hoary sanction of antiquity, is to be regarded as a self-evident falsehood, and at war with mankind.

Resolved, That the speedy success of our cause depends upon the zealous and untiring efforts of both men and women, for the overthrow of the monopoly of the pulpit, and for the securing to woman an equal participation with men in the various trades, professions, and commerce.

An Appeal to the Christian Women
of the South

. . . Why appeal to *women* on this subject? We do not make the laws which perpetuate slavery. No legislative power is vested in *us;* we can do nothing to overthrow the system, even if we wished to do so. To this I reply, I know you do not make the laws, but I also know that *you are the wives and mothers, the sisters, and daughters of those who do;* and if you really suppose that you can do nothing to overthrow slavery, you are greatly mistaken. You can do much in every way: four things I will name.

1. Read then on the subject of slavery. Read the *Bible* then, it contains the words of Jesus, and they are spirit and life. Judge for yourselves, whether he *sanctioned* such a system of oppression and crime.

2. Pray over this subject. When you have entered into your closets, and shut the doors, then pray to your father, who seeth in secret, that he would open your eyes to see whether slavery is *sinful,* and if it is, that he would make you to bear a faithful, open and unshrinking testimony against it, and to do whatsoever your hands find to do, leaving the consequences entirely to him, who still says to us, whenever we try to reason away duty from the fear of consequences, *"What is that to thee, follow thou me."*

3. Speak on this subject. It is through the tongue, the pen and the press, that truth is principally propagated. Speak then

to your relatives, your friends, your acquaintances on the subject of slavery; be not afraid if you are conscientiously convinced it is *sinful,* to say so openly, but calmly, and to let your sentiments be known. Above all, try to persuade your husband, father, brother, and sons, that *slavery is a crime against God and man,* and that it is a great sin to keep *human beings* in such abject ignorance, to deny them the privilege of learning to read and write . . .

4. Act on this subject. Some of you *own* slaves yourselves. If you believe slavery is *sinful* set them at liberty, "undo the heavy burdens and let the oppressed go free." If they wish to remain with you, pay them wages, if not let them leave you. Should they remain teach them, and have them taught the common branches of an English education; they have minds, and those minds *ought to be* improved.

But some of you will say, we can neither free our slaves nor teach them to read, for the laws of our state forbid it. Be not surprised when I say such wicked laws *ought to be no barrier* in the way of your duty, and I appeal to the Bible to prove this position . . .

The women of the North have engaged in this work [anti-slavery efforts] from a sense of *religious duty,* and nothing will ever induce them to take their hands from it until it is fully accomplished. They feel no hostility to you, no bitterness or wrath; they rather sympathize in your trials and difficulties; but they will know that the first thing to be done to help you, is to pour in the light of truth on your minds, to urge you to reflect on, and pray over the subject. This is all they can do for you; you must work out your own deliverance with fear and trembling, and with the direction and blessing of God, *you can do it* . . .

Chicago Declaration of Evangelical Social Concern

Adopted November 25, 1973

As evangelical Christians committed to the Lord Jesus Christ and the full authority of the Word of God, we affirm that God lays total claim upon the lives of his people. We cannot, therefore, separate our lives in Christ from the situation in which God has placed us in the United States and the world.

We confess that we have not acknowledged the complete claims of God on our lives.

We acknowledge that God requires love. But we have not demonstrated the love of God to those suffering social abuses.

We acknowledge that God requires justice. But we have not proclaimed or demonstrated his justice to an unjust American society. Although the Lord calls us to defend the social and economic rights of the poor and the oppressed, we have mostly remained silent. We deplore the historic involvement of the church in America with racism and the conspicuous responsibility of the evangelical community for perpetuating the personal attitudes and institutional structures that have divided the body of Christ along color lines. Further, we have failed to condemn the exploitation of racism at home and abroad by our economic system.

135

We affirm that God abounds in mercy and that he forgives all who repent and turn from their sins. So we call our fellow evangelical Christians to demonstrate repentance in a Christian discipleship that confronts the social and political injustice of our nation.

We must attack the materialism of our culture and the maldistribution of the nation's wealth and services. We recognize that as a nation we play a crucial role in the imbalance and injustice of international trade and development. Before God and a billion hungry neighbors, we must rethink our values regarding our present standard of living and promote more just acquisition and distribution of the world's resources.

We acknowledge our Christian responsibilities of citizenship. Therefore, we must challenge the misplaced trust of the nation in economic and military might—a proud trust that promotes a national pathology of war and violence which victimizes our neighbors at home and abroad. We must resist the temptation to make the nation and its institutions objects of near-religious loyalty.

We acknowledge that we have encouraged men to prideful domination and women to irresponsible passivity. So we call both men and women to mutual submission and active discipleship.

We proclaim no new gospel, but the Gospel of our Lord Jesus Christ who, through the power of the Holy Spirit, frees people to that righteousness which exalts a nation.

We make this declaration in the biblical hope that Christ is coming to consummate the Kingdom and we accept his claim on our total discipleship till he comes.[1]

(Women signers were Ruth Bentley, Sharon Gallagher, Nancy Hardesty, Wyn Wright Potter, Eunice Schatz and Donna Simons. Men whose names will be recognized are John F. Alexander, editor of *The Other Side,* Mark Hatfield, Lewis Smedes, and Ronald Sider.)

[1]Reprinted with permission of Evangelicals For Social Action, and from *The Chicago Declaration*, ed. Ronald J. Sider (Carol Stream, Ill.: Creation House, Inc., 1974).

Statement of Faith of Evangelical Women's Caucus

(It is possible that there will be a name change before you read this; it is being considered by the organization. But the statement of faith will be the same!)

We believe that God, the Creator and Ruler of all, has been self-revealed as the Trinity.

We believe that God created humankind, female and male, in the divine image, for fellowship with God and one another. We further believe that because of human sinful disobedience, the right relationship with God was shattered, with a consequent disruption of all other relationships.

We believe that God in love has made possible a new beginning through the Incarnation, in the life, death and resurrection of Jesus Christ, who was, and is, truly divine and truly human.

We affirm a personal relationship with Jesus Christ as Savior and Lord.

We believe that under Christ's headship and through the work of the Holy Spirit we are freed to exercise our rights responsibly in our churches, homes and society.

We believe that the Bible which bears witness to Christ is the Word of God, inspired by the Holy Spirit, and is the infallible guide and final authority for Christian faith and life.

We believe the church is the community of women and men who have been divinely called to fellowship with God and one another to seek and do God's will, looking forward to God's coming glorious kingdom.

Index

A

Adams, Abigail, 68
Adams, John Quincy, 28
Alcott, Louisa May, 31, 32, 33
All We're Meant to Be (Scanzoni and Hardesty), 96, 97
Allen, Rev. Jonathan, 40
American Anti-Slavery Society, 7
American Board of Commissioners for Foreign Missions (Congregational Church), 39
American Woman Suffrage Association, 55, 57
An Appeal in Favor of the Class of Americans Called Africans (Child), 9
Anthony, Susan B., 2, 3, 45, 46, 47, 54, 55, 56, 57, 72, 73
"Appeal to the Christian Women of the South" (Grimké A.), 9
Association of Women Ministers (Association of Women Preachers), 81

B

Beecher, Catherine, 63
Bethune, Joanna, 26
Bradbury, William, 27
Burnett, Mr., of Essex, 2
Bible Status of Women, The (Starr), 98
Bloomer, Amelia, 47, 61

N

O

P

R

S

U